Growing Up with Eddie

A Nostalgic Look at Being a Kid in the '70s

Nancy Golden

∾

For information or inquiries, email Nancy Golden at
nancy@goldencrossranch.com

Library of Congress Control Number: 2025923332

Published by Golden Cross Ranch LLC
Carrollton, Texas U.S.A.

Cover Design by Naomi Golden
www.naomigoldencreative.com

To Mom and Dad,
Thank you for the blessing of a wonderful childhood. I know you are watching from Heaven and can see the impact your love and hard work have made on my life, and in turn, a beautiful legacy for your grandkids and for generations to come. I'm sure you were happy to see Eddie, although we all sure do miss him down here. I couldn't have had a better brother to grow up with, and I am very grateful. I love you all.

This book is also dedicated to our kids: my son, Joshua, and Eddie's son, Joseph, and his daughters, Jessica and Kaylen. I hope you enjoy the stories shared here—that they give you a new perspective on what shaped us and how truly blessed we were. It is our hope that we have passed those blessings on to you.

The parents, teachers, and clergy who poured into us '70s kids deserve special recognition. Thank you for investing in us during our crucial formative years. And to my friend, April Holtzman, who created a '70s haven at Camp Tonkawa in Collinsville, TX—where kids can experience the same independence and freedom we did growing up.

And finally, to the kids of the '70s in Richardson and beyond. We grew up in a very special time. I hope this book helps you to treasure your own memories of what was home in your youth.

Contents

Foreword

Growing up in Richardson, Texas, in the '70s was a classic childhood adventure. When I think about my childhood, my most cherished memories are those focused on summertime activities with my brothers and our friends. From as early as four years old, I can remember hopping on my stylishly painted bicycle, expertly painted by my dad with blue and white spray paint, with my big brother, Steve (who was also friends with Eddie), tearing through the alleyways in search of adventures.

I only needed the training wheels for a day or two, and we were off spending our days collecting tadpoles and crawdads from neighborhood creeks with the only instructions being, "look both ways" and "come home when the streetlights come on." My mom tells the stories of our returning with every assortment of critters imaginable, from toads to turtles to snakes, lovingly placed in discarded containers or bulky pockets, and the plea, "Can I keep it?" In those days, Richardson was an area where civilization met the wild.

Summers were filled with flips from the high dive at Terrace Pool and continued creek explorations, traveling through water canals that were always referred to as creeks. They would take us through neighborhoods, under the town's streets and byways, until we would pop up across town in a park or some undeveloped area; destinations we would never be able to achieve were we restricted to travel by road.

As we grew, I developed other interests, traded my bike in for a horse, and traveled the undeveloped areas on horseback. Just two blocks from our house was the "big city of Buckingham." Buckingham was an independent city made up of two streets of houses nestled within Richardson, each having 2-3 acres of land zoned for livestock. I kept a horse at someone's house for twenty bucks a month and worked to support the upkeep of my faithful steed. Even so, I still managed to play basketball for the Richardson Jr High School Falcons and later for the Berkner Rams.

Author, Nancy "P'scetti" Venetucci Golden, and I share many Richardson life experiences as we played city league soccer for the Blue Racers, conquered many youth group adventures with Berkner football coach, turned youth minister, Edd Eason, and of course...the horse shenanigans. Sadly, our riding trails gradually became housing, apartments, and businesses. The city of Buckingham was developed into a string of liquor stores. Progress can be crushing. They say you can never go back, and I suppose that's true in a way.

Still, many things in Richardson have remained, and, of course, we'll always have the memories! And thanks to my childhood friend, P'scetti, many of those memories are recorded for us to enjoy in Growing Up with Eddie. We now have a book we can also share with our kids and grandkids (and future generations) and give them a glimpse of what it meant to be a kid growing up in the '70s.

— Katherine Deans Evanson,
 Foreign Service Medical Officer / Richardson Kid

Introduction

Whenever we complained to Mom about taking our picture, she would smile and say, "Someday you'll be glad I did." As usual, she was right... I am so grateful for the pictures you will find sprinkled throughout these pages. Thanks, Mom!!

Eddie and Nancy standing in front of their house on Rorary Drive in Richardson, Texas; author photo

My beloved big brother Eddie Venetucci died battling pancreatic cancer this past March (2025). I dedicated the final book, Key of Power, in my fantasy trilogy to him (it was released in March, and I am grateful he got to see it right before the Lord called him home). I would like to share the dedication here:

> *To my big brother and forever friend,*
> *Eddie Venetucci.*
> *Having a brother is wonderful! It means always having someone cheering you on and being understood and loved for all eternity.*
> *Eddie, your love and care for our family and your compassion and nurturing nature for others is a blessing and an inspiration for all of us. I am so grateful God picked me to be your baby sister. You'll always be my Maytag repairman. Much love always.*

Hint: You'll understand the Maytag repairman reference after reading *The Famous Dryer Incident.*

I was struggling about what to write next and planned on taking a sabbatical from writing until January, but childhood memories were uppermost on my mind, so I started my next book, a nostalgic look at growing up in the '70s in Richardson, Texas. A title immediately came to mind: "Growing Up with Eddie."

Until his death, Eddie was the last person (besides me) to live in our house on Rorary Drive near Terrace Elementary who experienced my childhood home, and I feel driven to record the stories that will die with me if I don't write them down.

The sad thing is, I don't have a good memory (Eddie

Introduction

remembered everything!), but I was blessed to spend a lot of time with Eddie during his last year with us. We talked, laughed, cried, prayed, and shared memories, so all is not lost.

It was such an idyllic time, and I know many of you share the same feelings about your childhood. My dad died in 1978 when I was two months shy of turning fifteen (and our world changed completely), and so the time period I will be writing about is from 1969-1978.

I am basically writing a series of vignettes—some fun, some poignant, some snapshots of special events, that are reminiscent of the childhood Eddie and I shared.

Writing these stories has made a deep impression on me. It has been both cathartic, emotional, awe-inspiring, and hopeful. Cathartic as I work through my grief of saying goodbye to my beloved brother, emotional as it has driven home that I am the only one left from our household on Rorary Drive, awe-inspiring when I reflect on the depth of love and care our parents devoted to Eddie and I during our childhood, and renewed hope in the wonderful response I have received from my fellow kids of the '70s during the creation of this book.

Next is a Facebook post I wrote recently after returning to my old neighborhood in Richardson to do some research:

Introduction

Nancy having lunch at the iconic Del's Charcoal Burgers on McKinney St in Richardson, TX; author photo

Okay, folks, I'm back from our field trip to Richardson. For those of you just now catching up—I am an author, and the book that I am working on is "Growing Up with Eddie," a nostalgic look at growing up in Richardson with my brother in the '70s.

Imagine my surprise when we took the Arapaho Rd exit off of 75 and turned onto Arapaho, only to see our beloved library surrounded by fences due to construction. I did not know it was being remodeled. Fortunately, we found the new, albeit temporary, location. Stacey Davis, the Librarian who focuses on local history, was very helpful. She is searching for some photos for the book and hopefully will find some.

Our jaunt around Richardson was both enjoyable and emotional. A stop at Terrace Park brought smiles and tears.

Introduction

From my adult perspective, it's not nearly as big as when I was a kid. The fence separating the school grounds and Terrace Swimming Pool was nonexistent when we were growing up. The baseball field looked a little sad, grass shrubs peeking through the red dirt of the infield. I walked up to the chain link fence, where I could see home plate, and envisioned my brother Eddie playing baseball. I could just picture him yanking his catcher's mask off as he held his baseball glove skyward to catch a pop fly. That's when the tears came...

We went by what is no longer Richardson Junior High, but the steps to the front doors that I rode my horse up were still there. We drove around to the back of the school—after my dad had died, I used to skip class and sit out there sometimes. It didn't quite look the same as I remembered.

We drove up and down the streets where Eddie and I shared a paper route for the Richardson Daily News. We drove down the alley between Rorary and Terrace that I used to walk to go to Terrace Swimming Pool. Peering through the fence, I could see the pool but didn't see any sign of a high or low diving board.

We drove down Belt Line and pulled over to get a picture of the railroad tracks that are suspended over Belt Line at Bowser, with traffic whizzing underneath. We rode our horses across that bridge when I was in junior high, and it looked just like it did back then. Hubby couldn't believe I did something that crazy. Next, lunch at Del's. Of course, I had to get a root beer in a frosty mug.

All that said, it's really true—you can't go home again. But you can treasure the memories of what was home. And that's what we'll be doing together in "Growing Up with Eddie."

Disclaimer

Not every memory may be accurate, but they are as accurate as I can remember. For some, I really wish Eddie were here to ask for specific details—he had a great memory—but I am sure he is smiling from heaven at my efforts.

∼

You may notice the lack of names when describing people and events, even to the point that it is a bit awkward. This is intentional, not because I don't remember their names and wouldn't have been delighted to mention the wonderful people that crossed our paths, but because of copyright laws.

If I have not been able to contact the person mentioned, while I should be able to legally mention them because everyone I write about is portrayed in a positive light, there is no law against frivolous lawsuits, which can quickly become a very expensive proposition. Due to these unfortunate circumstances, I have chosen to err on the side of caution and not name anyone unless I have been able to specifically get their permission.

~

Photos are used with permission and credit given to their source. A pencil sketch/drawing style has been applied to each photo, but no photo in this book has been AI-generated. Style transfer used by Lunapic, the platform I used to convert the photos to drawings, modifies the existing photo rather than generating a new image from scratch. From my inquiry to Lunapic: "We're using older tech, not ai generated."

I am using drawings instead of the actual photographs for two reasons: in some instances, the photographs, due to their age, actually look better as black and white drawings, and I think the drawings give the book a more "vintage" quality to its pages, fitting for stories that take place in the '70s.

Please forgive me in that some of the details in the drawings may be difficult to discern; these are very old pictures and it also has to do with the resolution of the original photographs.

I hope you enjoy them!

Terrace Elementary

"Nance, quit procrastinating and eat your cereal. You'll be late for school!" I could hear my mom's voice urging me to get going as I sat at our dining room table reading the back of my Quisp cereal box. She had already taken a brush to my unruly curly hair and packed my peanut butter and jelly sandwich, baggie of potato chips, Little Debbie snack cake, and thermos of milk into my Peanuts-themed lunchbox with Snoopy and Woodstock. I shoved a few more spoons of cereal into my mouth, looked around to make sure mom wasn't watching, and picked up the bowl in two hands and gulped down the rest. I wiped away my milk mustache and jumped up from the table.

Running to my mom, I wrapped my arms around her for a quick hug. "Thanks, Mom, I'm going. Love you!"

Nancy Golden

Nancy riding her bicycle on her driveway; author photo

I grabbed my lunchbox and the homework assignments I had brought with me to breakfast and ran out the back door, then down the steps. I put my lunchbox and my homework folder in the basket of my bicycle and rode it out the front gate of our backyard, down the driveway, and into the street in front of our house on Rorary Drive.

Terrace Elementary School; author photo

Living just a block from Terrace Elementary, the only busy street I had to cross was Dorothy, directly in front of the school. The principal, Mr. West, was outside watching over the morning rush. I rode to the bike racks and shoved my bike into one of the slots, grabbed my lunchbox and folder, and ran inside.

Locating my locker, I quickly opened it, grabbed my notebook, and ran to my homeroom, sliding into my seat just before the bell rang. Catching my breath, I skimmed the essay I had written the night before, along with the math problems I had answered. I noticed a mistake and grabbed a pencil out of the cigar box I had under my seat. I hurriedly erased the wrong answer and replaced it with the right one just as the announcement to stand for the pledge resounded through the school. I stood up with my classmates, placed my hand over my heart, and recited the Pledge of Allegiance. It was a comforting, almost sacred, way to start the day.

Easter parade at Terrace Elementary; author photo

Every holiday was a special event and celebrated at school. I remember in third grade, I had a crush on a boy. Easter was approaching, and we were told that we would be participating in an Easter parade. We were expected to wear our Sunday best, and imagine my joy when I found out I was paired with him (apparently because we were the same height) to walk together during the parade! Instructions were sent home with the girls on how to make an Easter bonnet, which my mom dutifully purchased the supplies for: light blue crepe paper and little easter ornaments to adorn the paper plate that would serve as the bonnet. I had the biggest smile, holding hands with my crush. He didn't say much, but then none of the boys did.

On another occasion, in sixth grade, we were going to have a Christmas party (which we did every year). I was so excited! Mom bought me a white dress with red trim, and I felt so pretty. I was usually a tomboy and loved to play street hockey in the Terrace Elementary School parking lot. I was also good enough at soccer that the boys would let me play soccer with them at recess. But I really liked a boy in my class (who didn't know I existed), and I thought he might notice me at the Christmas party.

The party was scheduled for the last period of school, and in our classroom, the parents had brought in a large punch bowl with red punch, along with lots of Christmas cookies. Somehow, I sloshed the punch that was in my cup, and it splashed all over the front of my beautiful white dress, a red stain spreading across it. Horrified, I burst into tears and ran out of the classroom. My sixth-grade heart was shattered as the red punch made its way down my Christmas outfit.

I ran to my bike in the bicycle racks in front of the school and rode it the short ride home, bawling my eyes out. That was probably the most traumatic incident of my elementary school years. Eddie found me, eyes red from crying, and did what he always did when I was upset. He asked me who made me cry. He was not going to allow his baby sister to be bullied. When I told him what happened, he just shook his head, gave me a hug, and told me to forget about it.

Growing Up with Eddie

Big brother Eddie and baby sister Nancy; author photo

Which reminds me of a time when I was really being bullied. A few doors down, two brothers lived on our street. The older one was a couple of years older than Eddie and the oldest kid on our block of Rorary Drive. He liked to act tough and boss us around. One day, he went too far in teasing me and made me cry. I ran down the sidewalk to our house, where Eddie was playing with some of the neighborhood kids. He asked me what happened, and I told him the boy was mean to me. Eddie didn't even take a minute to think of the consequences of attacking the much larger, stronger bully of the block. He ran over to him, swinging, yelling at him to leave his sister alone. Eddie willingly got beaten up that day, defending me. That was the kind of brother he was.

Lunch with Daddy

Winning lunch tray; courtesy RetroDivaBoutique /
ebay.com

I remember one day my dad came to my elementary school to have lunch with me. I was so happy!! We picked up our trays to go through the cafeteria line. That day, we were having chicken-fried steak patties. Lunch was fifty cents, but if your tray had an X on it, you got your meal for free. That was something the school did just for fun. I was so excited—it was the first (and I think only time) I had picked up the tray with an X on it. Imagine that—on the same day my dad was visiting during lunch...

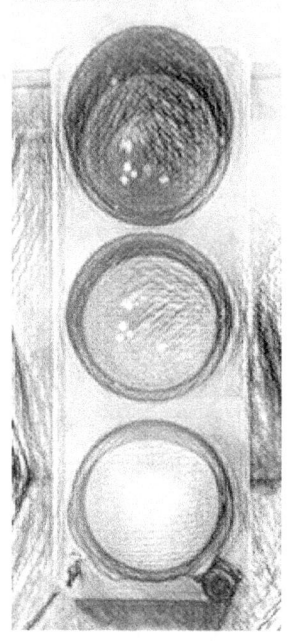

Traffic light regulating noise level in Terrace cafeteria; courtesy cha-ching30290 / ebay.com

I was so proud sitting next to my dad at the long tables in our school cafeteria. I remember explaining to him about the big traffic light that was easily visible on one of the tables in the center. Green meant we could talk normally, yellow meant we needed to whisper or quiet down, and red meant no talking at all. The noise level rose and fell as we talked and kept an eye on the traffic light. We ate lunch together, and Dad let me keep my two quarters. It was a very special day all around!

The Ferret Caper

My friend Katherine and I had many adventures together. She lived on Highland Blvd, so she was about a one-mile bike ride away. Granny dresses were popular at the time and went down to our ankles. Once I decided to ride my bike to her house while wearing one. That was probably the most uncomfortable ride of my life, hitching up my red dress with yellow flowers so it wouldn't get caught in the spokes. I always thought it great fun that whenever I went inside Katherine's house, inevitably a cockatiel would land on my head.

Katherine and I shared a love of animals, which often influenced our time together. We frequently visited Pet World, and I became a thorn in that pet shop's side that followed me into young adulthood. Let me explain:

Mom and Dad went on vacation to Mexico without us. They decided Eddie and I were old enough to stay alone, especially since our married older sister lived in the apartment complex that was at the end of our street (the apartment complex directly behind Terrace Shopping Center). While they were gone, Eddie and I enjoyed our freedom. I took my saved-up allowance and Katherine took hers, and we rode our bikes to Pet World, where we bought a ferret.

Jake the ferret; courtesy Serena Koi / pexels.com

Ferrets are very interesting creatures; they are members of the weasel family and, from our perspective, furry and cute. We took that ferret everywhere. He did a really good job of staying cuddled under our shirts when we wanted to hide him in a store that didn't allow pets, and would stay in my jacket when I was riding my bike—his head sticking out the front of it. We had a few glorious days with our newfound buddy—until Mom and Dad got home.

Now, I have to admit that our ferret (named Jake) was not the best-smelling of pets and was rather messy. That was probably a factor in my mom's response. Needless to say, she was not happy. Informing her that Katherine owned half was not helpful. Mom insisted that we return Jake to Pet World.

However, this was not easily accomplished. Pet World did not want Jake back. But my mom was determined. The area manager happened to be there, and very reluctantly, she took Jake back to his cage and refunded our money. We were very sad to see Jake go, and as I recall, we weren't very welcome at Pet World after that. This was the location in Richardson, in the same shopping center as Kroger and Baskin-Robbins at Belt Line Road near Plano Road.

So, fast forward about ten years. I was working at Kroger on Forest Lane and wanted to get a second part-time job in the area. I saw a Pet World at Preston and Forest, so I decided to apply. As it turned out, it was the same people who owned the Richardson store. Not only that, the same area manager was there the day I applied. She didn't remember me, which was a good thing.

Pet World Policy; Canva author design

I did get the job, and I had to keep a straight face when she started explaining all of the rules, and got to the Pet World policy on refunds. She mentioned that a kid bought a ferret a few years ago while her parents were on vacation, and when the parents returned, they were furious. Pet World had to take the ferret back (which is always a questionable thing to do because you never know what the people did while they had the animal and what it might have been exposed to). So, after that day, they made a rule that no one under 18 was allowed to purchase any live animals.

I never shared with her that I was that kid. I figured that was on a need-to-know basis...

Alto Sax

Eddie practicing in his bedroom; author photo

Since my bedroom was next door to his, I would hear
Eddie playing scales on his alto saxophone. He worked
hard at learning to play well and became quite good.

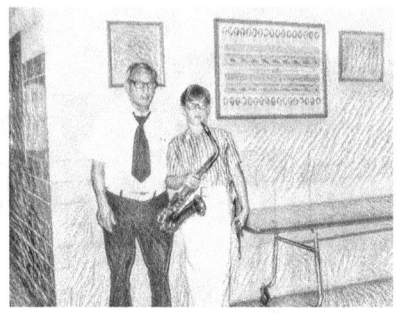

Dad with Eddie at a band concert; author photo

We always enjoyed coming to school for our band concerts. I played clarinet, but it was soon obvious to all that I did not need to pursue it. Eddie, on the other hand, had a real musical gift.

Eddie in his marching band uniform; author photo

Growing Up with Eddie

Mom was very proud of Eddie's musical accomplishments;
author photo

Eddie practiced most days and went on many fun band trips. When he got to Berkner, he was in marching band.

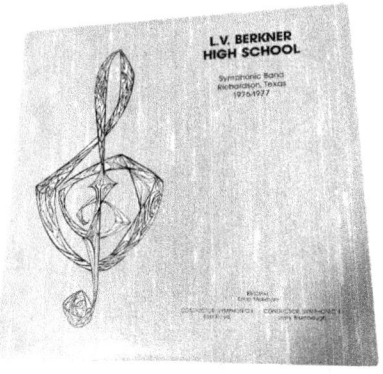

Album cover of L.V. Berkner High School Orchestra with
Eddie's alto sax solo; author photo

Being a member of the Berkner Ram Marching Band was a very special and important part of his life. He got to play an alto sax solo on the band record album—we were all so proud of that accomplishment!

He made many lifelong friends in band and had a positive impact on those around him, especially on the younger band members who were finding their way. Eddie continued serving others all of his life—he spent much of his time volunteering in church activities and with community organizations, including the Garland Citizen Police and Fire Academies.

Random Snippets of Around Town

So many memories!

Next Door Restaurant: Eddie and I loved to eat there! We would take turns calling in our order on the telephone and always ordered Suzy Q fries.

~

Ponchos Mexican Buffet was also a favorite. Being able to raise the flag to get more food was so fun, and Eddie and I both loved the sopapillas.

~

Gibson's department store was often our destination when shopping for household items. One time, they had a raffle, and Mom entered. The manager called her at home to tell her the news—she had won the bicycle they had on display—we were all so excited!

Dad loved to eat at Bonanza, I think because it fit in with his love of everything cowboy. His business fluctuated quite a bit during the years. Some months it would be flourishing and the money seemed to be rolling in, at other times it seemed we were barely scraping by. If we ate at Bonanza, we were flourishing.

The western decor suited me—reminding me of horses. The salad bar was a new experience. It was so much fun filling our salad bowls with our choices! Mom would always get the bleu cheese dressing, so I did, too. Not being used to eating steak, I would get a hamburger and wide steak fries. I can't remember what Eddie got, but I am guessing he went for a steak and baked potato since he was older. I remember being astounded once, watching Dad pay for our meal for four. To me, it was the height of extravagance to spend so much money on one meal.

Everyone loved going to Olla Podrida. The indoor market with shops on two levels and rickety wooden stairs to get to the top level ones was just plain fun. Mom had given me a printer's tray, and there was a shop that carried miniatures that were perfect for putting into its small spaces. I loved it when Mom took me there to get a new figurine. Miniature ceramic figures competed with small plastic Coca-Cola bottles for a space in the tray hanging on my wall.

Echols Feed Store off of Main Street was a frequent destination for me on my bicycle, even before I had a horse. The store represented my dream to have my own horse one day, and I loved picking up a piece of tack and daydreaming about buying it. I bought my first hoof pick from there.

Murphy's Clinic on Greenville Avenue was the vet clinic that Mom took our pets to when needed, and was established in the early '70s. It was always a comforting, familiar landmark whenever I drove back into Richardson.

Richardson icon: Del's Charcoal Burgers; author photo

I ate at Del's recently as part of my research for "Growing Up with Eddie." Locals assured me it hasn't changed a bit, and I found my burger and frosty root beer delicious. I am guessing I didn't eat there in the '70s (that I can remember) because we lived so close to Dairy Queen in the Terrace Shopping Center, and that was our destination for a Hunger Buster, vanilla custard cone, or Dilly Bar. Eddie went to work there when he was old enough, which was an added bonus since we got his employee discount.

Parades

Richardson Centennial parade. 1973 - Terrace
Elementary float; courtesy Richardson Public Library

Richardson always had Christmas and Fourth of July
parades when Eddie and I were growing up. We
would go to Dairy Queen for a Dilly Bar and then
line the streets of Greenville Avenue in front of Terrace Shopping Center to watch, or sometimes we were active partici-

pants. Small town community was never sweeter as the parade wound its way down Belt Line Rd and through town, families standing shoulder to shoulder, waving and smiling as local organizations, businesses, or just kids and adults wanting to be a part, marched down the center of the street, often tossing candy to the children standing on the curb who were clapping and cheering.

One year, Eddie and I decorated our bicycles for the Fourth of July parade. First, we took the garden hose and made a bucket of soapy water to wash our Schwinn bikes. When they were shiny clean and dried in the hot Texas sun, we attached red, white, and blue streamers to the handlebars, and weaved them through the spokes. We joined other Richardson kids riding their bikes in the parade. So much fun!

Later that year, I joined my Girl Scout troop in the Christmas parade. We were all dressed as Christmas boxes: individual large cardboard boxes we had each decorated with Christmas wrapping paper and bows. We marched in the parade with our heads poking out the top and our arms poking out the sides.

Richardson Centennial Celebration.1973 - Horses in parade; courtesy Richardson Public Library

Another year, when I had my horse, Cindy, I decided to ride in the Fourth of July parade with the other kids on horseback—a Richardson tradition. I made a red, white, and blue Uncle Sam hat, which perched on Cindy's head, her ears poking through the holes I had made for them. I was wearing matching red, white, and blue—my shirt was blue with red and white piping on the sleeves, and white pants—sort of.

My pants had not fared well when I went to the barn to get Cindy saddled and ready. I had brushed her out the day before and brought her up to stay in a paddock so I could catch her easily for the parade. Unfortunately, it had rained enough to turn the dirt in the paddock into mud, and Cindy had decided to roll. She was encrusted in mud when I arrived on parade day, and I had no choice—she needed a bath.

By the time I got her cleaned up with the barn water hose, my pants were soaked and had turned gray. I was still excited to ride in the parade, and it was a nice, warm, sunny day, so I soon dried off. I forgot all about my morning mishap in the excitement of riding Cindy and waving to friends and family. It was my first parade on horseback, and I was so proud to be a part! I had a great time, and it was even more memorable because of how it started.

Cowboy Boots and Weights

I often accompanied my mom to her job at Myer's Department store in Terrace Shopping Center, especially during Christmas break. Upon our arrival, I would head to the back of the store to the employee break room. Waiting for me there was a long table and a couple of chairs. On top of the table was a large coffee can filled with well-worn crayons, many of the paper labels peeled off, and a couple of coloring books. A Coca-Cola bottle vending machine made its home in one corner. I would settle myself into a chair and grab a handful of crayons to choose from for my artwork.

Mom would go about her work in women's clothing, coming by occasionally to check on me. I was horse-crazy from a very young age, and besides coloring, I often drew horses on the paper my mom scrounged from the manager's office for my artistic efforts.

The manager was always very nice to me, although I was a little scared of him. He was very big (at least to my elementary school-sized self), and had a deep voice, which made him seem stern. I loved going into his office because the clock on the wall looked like a black cat, and its tail would swing.

One day, while I was coloring, my mom entered the break room with a smile.

"Nance, I need your help."

Now, that had never happened before, and I was quite excited to be a big girl and help my mother with her job. I jumped up and dutifully followed her to the children's shoe department. Several racks of shoes filled with pretty dress shoes and tennis shoes were on display.

We usually got my shoes at Kmart, so I was very curious about why my mom wanted me in the shoe department. My head was turning this way and that, taking in all of the merchandise that surrounded us, when another lady walked up.

Mom put her hands on my shoulders. "This is my daughter, Nancy."

The other lady smiled. "Why, thank you for agreeing to help us, Nancy."

I turned to my mother with a puzzled look on my face. She gazed down at me with a serious expression. "This lady is buying her daughter a pair of cowboy boots for Christmas. She wants it to be a surprise, so she can't have her try them on." Mom looked over at the woman and winked. "It just so happens you are the exact same size as her daughter. We thought it would be really nice if you could try on the boots, so she can make sure she is buying the correct size."

Now that seemed like a perfectly reasonable request, so I smiled at my mom and nodded my head. Mom pointed to the chair that was set out for trying on shoes, and I plopped into it. She brought over a rather large box that contained a pair of bright, shiny black cowboy boots with multi-colored stitching. She set them in front of my chair, and I pulled each boot on.

"They feel good," I said hesitantly, wishing they were for me, but way too conscious of our family's finances to say that out loud. I didn't want my mom to feel bad that they weren't going to be mine.

Mom looked down at me with an expression on her face that I couldn't quite fathom. She nodded. "That's good, but you'd better walk in them just to make sure."

I obediently took a couple of laps around the shoe department while the grownups watched. I returned and sat back in the chair. I directed my gaze at the other lady, waiting for my verdict. "Since your daughter is my size, I think they'll be perfect," I announced.

"Wonderful," she replied, her face breaking into a big smile. "Thank you for helping me. You are a very sweet little girl."

I looked down shyly and mumbled, "Thank you."

Mom patted my shoulder. "Thanks, Nance. You can take them off now so I can put them away for the other little girl."

I nodded and slipped off the boots. I handed them back to my mom, who took them and put them back in the box.

"Go on back to the breakroom and color some more. I still have thirty minutes left to work."

"Okay, Mom." I got up and wandered through the store and back to the breakroom. My mind dwelt on the beautiful boots and the lucky girl who would be getting them for Christmas. I was glad that I could help. *Maybe someday I'll get a pair of boots like that.* I went back to coloring and soon forgot about trying on the boots.

The days flew by, filled with Eddie and me watching Frosty the Snowman, Rudolph the Red-Nosed Reindeer, and the Peanuts Christmas special while eating Jiffy Pop popcorn.

CHRISTMAS DAY:

I had on my yellow robe with red and blue flowers sprinkled across the fabric. Eddie's robe was blue and white plaid with a Dallas Cowboys logo. We made a beeline to the kitchen and grabbed the plain brown paper bag on the counter. Opening it up, we took turns digging through the bagels inside, purchased the day before from Bagelstein's. We each grabbed one and toasted them, then slathered them with cream cheese. Contentedly munching on our bagels while waiting for Mom and Dad to make their entrance, we eyed the presents that we had already shamelessly scouted when Mom and Dad were out of the house—they had been hidden under their bed. Eddie would go so far as to unwrap his and take a peek before taping them back up. I could never bring myself to go that far, although I had no compunction about holding the ones with my name and rattling them to see if I could guess the contents. Mom was very smart, and this year, she foiled Eddie's plans and used newspaper so that he couldn't undo the wrapping—since the newspaper would tear if he tried!

Eddie and Nancy checking out the presents under the tree; author photo

Dad took his place sitting on the thin carpeting of our den, and me and Eddie picked out our spots on the floor, far enough apart to allow enough room to stack our beautifully wrapped presents around us. Mom sat on a chair, watching over the proceedings. As he did each year, Dad picked up one present at a time, looked at the tag for the name of the recipient, and either slid or tossed the package to them. Eddie and I caught our packages and put them in front of us, our faces glowing with happy anticipation at the prospect of opening them.

We knew there would be a mix of practical gifts with some fun ones, and once they were all handed out (including the gifts we got for Mom and Dad and the ones they got for each other), merry chaos ensued as we all dug in and started unwrapping our gifts, the air punctuated with joyful shrieks as we tore apart the paper and could view the treasure beneath. In my stack, Shrinky Dinks competed with a horse book, "The Album of Horses," and a Lite-Brite. I was so happy; I couldn't imagine any better presents.

Nancy's cowboy boots for Christmas; author photo

I had saved the biggest box for last and began to unwrap it.

Nancy Golden

I tore the Christmas paper off to find an oversized shoe box. I lifted the lid and to my amazement—there was a bright, shiny new pair of black cowboy boots with multi-colored stitching. I was so excited! I took them out of the box, immediately put them on my feet, and started jumping up and down in excitement. I was quite a sight in my yellow flower-speckled robe and black cowboy boots, my face radiant with joy. Mom watched me, smiling. What a sweet memory I have, of my mother carefully planning and carrying out her ruse so that I could be surprised on Christmas Day!

But there is more to the story...

One year (over 50 years later), I was trying to decide between two necklaces that I thought my mom would like for Christmas. Carrying forth my mom's tradition of Christmas surprises, I sent her an email, describing my dilemma but using an imaginary person in an effort to disguise my attempt to have her pick her own present. I wrote, "I am shopping for a present and wanted your opinion - which one do you think is prettier and would go with more outfits? The person it is for has similar tastes in jewelry and clothes as you do. Please let me know."

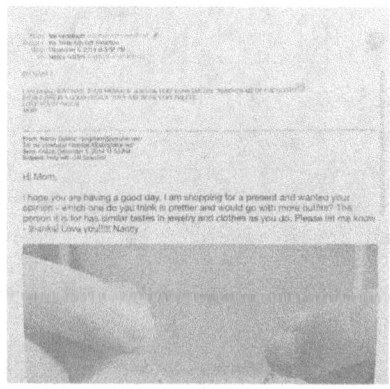

Emails between Nancy and Mom; author photo

30

And her response, "Your message sounds very familiar LOL. Reminds me of the boots 😊 Either one is a good choice. They are both very pretty."

As you can see, I couldn't fool my mom!

~

Eddie's weights for Christmas; author photo

Eddie also had quite a surprise. He had been looking forward to the bonanza of Christmas presents that he had snooped and found. Awaiting him were several boxes wrapped in newspaper. He opened the first box and pulled out two weights, the kind that would go onto the end of a pole used for weightlifting. He didn't realize for a while that they were all going to be weights, as every box contained weights for his new weight set. He was delighted to get what he was hoping for and thought it was really funny.

Next up were our stockings, hanging on the wall. Mom got them down and handed them to us. While the contents varied from year to year, one thing never failed: we got a Life Saver candy book that was filled with rolls of different flavors of Life Savers.

The Rocket Park

Fourth of July was always celebrated at our house growing up. My parents had a deep appreciation for America, since they both came from families that emigrated here. We also had several family members (including my dad) who had served our country. Mom always made sure we flew our flag on patriotic holidays.

Nancy on the radar dish at Heights Park; author photo

Usually, the Fourth meant we got to have a bucket of Kentucky Fried Chicken with the side fixin's—a rare treat for us! Mom would pack a blanket, Dad would get our ice chest ready, and we would pile into the car to head over to Heights Park for a picnic.

Eddie and Nancy in the rocket at Heights Park; author photo

Nancy playing on Saturn at Heights Park; author photo

We loved climbing up the giant rocket (although the metal slide would get really hot and burn us pretty good!) and the other space-themed play ground equipment. We also enjoyed playing in the creek. Eddie taught me how to pick out a flat rock and skip rocks in that creek. I got pretty good at it, and we would have contests to see who could get the most skips.

Roller Skating and Miniature Golf

Thunderbird Roller Rink! Going to the counter and asking for skates in your size, then hurriedly lacing them up so you could get out on the rink. Laboriously skating on the carpet to get to one of the entrances, where you could time it to pop onto the skating rink floor without crashing into anyone. The music suddenly stops, and silence prevails as everyone waits expectantly. Finally, the DJ calls out, "Come on to the center, everyone, it's time to do the 'Hokey Pokey!'"

Kids all swarm toward the center, some grabbing onto the nearest person to steady themselves. Finally, everyone gets lined up, and the music starts again. "Put your left foot in, then put your left foot out..."

The evening progresses with a variety of music and flashing lights in between regular skating time. "Boys only!" then "Girls only!" Then "couples only!" Kids go to the snack counter to get a Coke or a candy bar. Good times!

∾

We also enjoyed skating outdoors with roller skates and skate boards. I had a pair of metal skates that fit around my tennis shoes to skate down the sidewalk in front of our house and a blue plastic skateboard that I would use to roam around our neighborhood.

≈

*Twin Rivers Miniature Golf Course 1972 - Richardson
Daily News; courtesy Richardson Public Library*

Twin Rivers was the ultimate date/youth group/family destination. We played putt-putt golf, the arcade games, and tried our hand at the batting cages (Eddie's favorite). It was such a beautiful setting on a warm summer evening.

The Famous Dryer Incident

"Hey, this is fun!" Eddie poked his head out of the circular opening, the rest of his stocky body perched inside the Maytag dryer that lived inside our kitchen, across from the washing machine. His unruly brown hair and thick-framed glasses couldn't hide the sparkle in his eyes. He looked at me with his characteristically mischievous grin, and from past experience, I knew he was up to something.

He climbed out of the dryer, grin firmly in place. "You try it. Get in—It's fun!"

I gazed at my big brother, my lips pressed together in suspicion. Thinking it over, I finally replied, "No way! You'll turn it on!"

Eddie managed a look of hurt innocence; the same one he had perfected from a very young age. "No, I won't, I promise!" he replied.

I glanced around the kitchen, trying to decide what to do. The small wooden plaque that hung on the wall behind the washer, "The Kitchen Will Be Closed Today Because of

Illness—I'm Sick of Cooking," made me smile, as it always did. I shook my head and returned my attention to my brother, swinging the dryer door back and forth in anticipation.

I took a deep breath and stared intently into his eyes.

"You promise?"

"Yes, I promise!"

"Okay."

Maytag dryer; author photo

Eddie held the door open so that I could easily climb into the waiting abyss. I gripped the edges of the opening and wriggled inside. The metal was not very comfortable, and there wasn't much room with the plastic fins as I squatted inside and peeked out the opening, my hands still holding the edges.

"Awww, come on," Eddie encouraged. "Let go, so I can close the door."

"No!!"

"Awwww, come on. It'll be fun. You'll see."

"No. You'll turn it on," my voice wavered slightly.

Sensing my uncertainty, Eddie looked at me with big eyes and a reassuring smile.

"No, I won't. Go on, get all the way in. I'll just close the door for a second."

I narrowed my eyes at my big brother and cocked my head, considering his words. Hanging onto the edges was becoming uncomfortable, and it was tempting just to lean back and allow myself to fold my body into the dryer's drum.

"Okay. But don't turn it on!"

I turned loose of the edges and settled myself inside the dryer, squatting with my feet and hands pressed against the sides. Before I could change my mind, Eddie gleefully swung the door shut, and I was enveloped in darkness. I took a calming breath and shouted, "Remember, don't turn it on!" in case he forgot his promise.

A moment later, I heard the telltale noise that I associated with the dryer's timer being rotated, an action necessary for the dryer to begin rotating when the start button was depressed.

"EDDIE!!" I barely got out before I felt the motion of the drum beginning to turn, and I frantically grabbed the fins, pressing my feet as hard as I could against the metal drum's smooth surface. I was too busy trying to keep my position in the dryer stable to yell again, as the drum began to rotate. As I approached the roof of the inside of the dryer, I let go so that I wouldn't turn upside down and dropped to the bottom of the drum with a THUNK.

Eddie opened the dryer door, his action halting the dryer's rotation. He peered into the opening at me, jumbled up inside. His eyes were wide, and the mischievous grin was gone—and in its place a look of concern. "Are you okay?"

I glared at him as I scrambled out, shoving him out of the way.

"You could've killed me!"

"No, I wouldn't have kept it on. I just wanted to see what would happen."

"Well, what happened is that I rolled almost upside down inside it. It was scary!" My eyes grew moist, and a tear rolled down my cheek.

My big brother's shoulders dropped. He bit his lip and looked down at the floor. "I'm sorry," I heard him mutter. "Are you going to tell Mom?"

I gazed back at my brother. He was only a year and a half older than me and had always been in my corner. We fought daily as siblings do, yet we always had each other's backs. "Naaahhh," I sighed. "Just don't try that again!"

He looked up and grinned, his eyes sparkling again. How could I tattle on that mischievous face?

Little did I know at the time, the dryer incident would be forever immortalized in our family history when, years later, Eddie came to visit me at my first professional job as an engineer. The phone on my desk rang, and when I picked it up, the receptionist stationed in the lobby informed me in a puzzled voice, "The Maytag repairman is here to see you."

Bumper Pool Christmas and Silent Night

Eddie and Nancy on Christmas Day; author photo

O n Christmas Eve, we attended Midnight Mass at St. Paul's Church. When we got home, we were always allowed to pick one gift and open it before bed. Eddie and I would always get up early the next morning, in our bathrobes, and wait anxiously where Christmas was located each year in the Venetucci household.

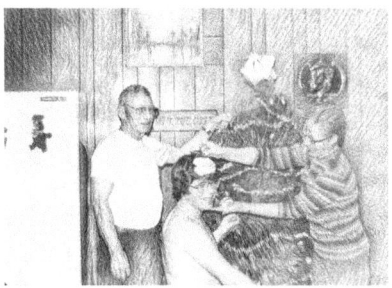

Mom, Dad, and Eddie, decorating the Christmas tree; author photo

Mom, Dad, and Nancy, decorating the Christmas tree; author photo

When we first moved into our house, the garage was being used as a stable for goats. My dad first converted it to an office for his company, R & L (Ralph & Lee) Sales, but it eventually became our family den. The two steps down from our dining room led into the holiday extravaganza—Mom loved decorating for Christmas. Decorating our Christmas tree was always a family affair, and placing the angel tree topper was a special moment.

Christmas tree with angel topper; author photo

The nativity scene under the Christmas tree; author photo

Dad would sit on the floor and go through the tangle of lights, replacing any burnt-out bulbs (back then, they were wired in series, so all of the bulbs had to be good for the lights to work) and wrapped them around the tree, saving a bulb for the nativity scene we put under it every year.

Eddie and Nancy with their Christmas stockings made by their neighbor; author photo

Mom would tape every single Christmas card we received on the wall, along with our Christmas stockings. Our next-door neighbor had made Eddie and me our very own stockings replete with sequins and cloth figures. A Bible, an angel, a Christmas tree, a train, a poodle, and a house adorned mine, with my name on it at the top in thin red tubes hand-sewn across the cuff. Eddie's stocking had a big, beautifully sequined Santa Claus across the front, along with a wreath and a present.

Bumper pool table with Christmas table cloth covering it;
author photo

One year, Mom found a bumper pool table on sale. She had it delivered while we were at school and placed it in the den. She put a piece of plywood across the top, which she covered with a colorful Christmas tablecloth. We had no idea it was there!

Christmas treats and Christmas cards; author photo

Mom had some traditional treats she put out every year. She usually put them on a card table where the bumper pool table was. This year, she disguised our very special Christmas present by loading it up with holiday treats, instead of pulling out the card table. The Christmas cards we received were taped to the wall behind it—adding to the festive look.

Santa's sleigh being pulled by Nancy's Breyer horses, author photo

I also contributed my Breyer horse collection and made a display of Santa's sleigh being pulled by a variety of horses.

Mom putting out holiday treats; author photo

Plastic plates in the shape of Santa Claus and a snowman held holiday candies: a variety of hard candy in ribbons and round and rectangular shapes of all colors, along with milk chocolate balls, and Santa and snowman-shaped chocolate wrapped in foil. A glass jar held an assortment of hard candy sticks. Italian sesame seed Regina cookies competed with Christmas sugar cookies on a decorative plate. A bowl containing mixed nuts (whoever ate those big brown ones?) had a nutcracker sitting conveniently next to it. We had no idea that the treat table was really a bumper pool table!

Eddie and Dad playing bumper pool; author photo

We were so excited when Mom revealed her surprise! The bumper pool table became the centerpiece of our den. It had red and white balls and was much smaller than a regular-sized pool table. We soon became experts at hitting all of the balls off the bumpers and into the opposing side's pockets.

Dad loved trains and another fun addition to our den was the train set Mom gave him for Christmas, one year. Dad got a large piece of plywood, put artificial grass on it, and laid out his track. I would go to Michael's and pick out a new train car or railroad sign to surprise him. Smoke would come out of the stack—we loved watching him run it!

~

Christmas tree with organ; author's photo

Mom and Dad enjoying Mom's Christmas present;
author photo

Another year, my dad decided to surprise my mom with an organ for Christmas. Mom loved to play, and it was so wonderful to see the happiness that gift brought. It was fairly large and took up a good portion of the den. With the press of a button, the keys could light up in different colors, marked with their notes. Dad also bought a music book that matched the notes with the keys so anyone could play a simple song. We all took turns playing it. Silent Night was a family favorite that we played every Christmas.

Family Visits

Through the years, family members would come to visit, and it was always a special time for all of us.

My two older brothers (Johnny and Vinny) were in the Air Force, so we didn't see them very often. When they came to visit, they made me feel like a princess. We had not grown up together, but it was comforting to know they were my big brothers.

My three older sisters, Fran (in New York), Lynn (in California), and Janet (in Texas), all married, would also visit occasionally. We always loved seeing Lynn and her son, Danny. Lynn was so excited when she found out Mom was having me, she convinced Mom to give me the same middle name as hers. We share the middle name—Carol.

Janet lived nearby, so we got to see her much more often, along with our nephews Wayne and Joshua, and our niece, Christy. It was wonderful having a big sister nearby growing up.

Eddie and Nancy with their niece Lori and nephew Walter; author photo

Fran had four kids when Eddie and I were growing up: Lori, Walter, Wendy, and Dennis. Jennifer and Sarah came later. One summer, Fran's two oldest kids (Lori and Walter) came to visit from New York, and we had a lot of fun showing them life in Texas.

Mom on left and Aunt Irene on right; author photo

We looked forward to my mom's sister, Aunt Irene, and her husband, Uncle Ike, coming to visit. She was very loving and was always ready for an adventure. Aunt Irene would bring us delicious knishes wrapped in foil from New York, and we usually got to go eat at Bagelstein's when they were in town. She was always my cheerleader and the first adult relative I conversed with about the deeper questions of life.

Eddie and Nancy with Aunt Theresa; author photo

Nancy and Dad with Aunt Theresa riding Fury; author photo

Our Aunt Theresa (Dad's sister) was very sweet and fun-loving. When she came to visit from where she lived in New York, she would ride bikes with me. She also went to the barn and rode Fury, the Shetland pony. Dad was so happy to be able to show his sister cowboy life.

Make a Wish

Thanksgiving at the Venetucci household; author photo

Through the years, Thanksgiving was always a special time of family. Mom would cook the traditional turkey with all of the sides. She would save the wishbone from the turkey and put it on a plate to dry. Dad would also make some special dishes.

A yearly ritual between me and Eddie would be for each of us to grasp the dried wish bone and make a wish.

"1, 2, 3, PULL!!"

We would each pull our end until the wishbone broke apart. Whoever got the larger end would have their wish come true.

Dad and Eddie always wanted a turkey leg. Mom always wanted breast meat. I liked it all. After our feast, Mom would put the leftover turkey in Tupperware and we made turkey and Miracle Whip sandwiches for the rest of the week.

Eddie and Nancy in their Thanksgiving outfits; author photo

We were often in school plays, and one year Eddie was dressed as a pilgrim. Holidays were so much fun growing up!

CB Radios and Leisure Suits and Bell Bottoms

"Captain Fantastic, this is KRV1110, the one and only P'scetti kid. Do you have your ears on?"

Smokey and the Bandit brought Citizen Band radios to the forefront of the public eye, and Dad decided to buy a base station and install an antenna. The radio found its home in Eddie's room, and we had a lot of fun picking out our handles.

Mom had beautiful red hair and decided her CB radio name would be "Carrot Top."

My friend Katherine once noted that little kids call spaghetti, "p'scetti"—and in a wink to my Italian heritage, my nickname became P'scetti (I am still called that to this day by my childhood friends) and my CB radio handle was "The P'scetti Kid."

Eddie settled on "Captain Fantastic," because he liked Elton John's music and thought it was a really cool name.

Being able to talk to people you didn't know was both exciting and awkward, and I was usually a little nervous. Eddie the extrovert was a natural and spent lots of time on the airwaves.

~

Dad and Eddie wearing their leisure suits; author photo

The '70s definitely had their own dress style; leisure suits were in fashion along with bell-bottoms.

*Eddie and Nancy with Dad in front of his Plymouth
Fury; author photo*

Here we are standing in front of Dad's Plymouth Fury. It was
dark green with a black hard top. And of course, we are all
dressed in '70s fashion.

The Bunny Rabbit

Mom with Nancy's parakeet on her shoulder; author photo

I was not only horse-crazy, but I also loved all animals, and a parade of pets were part of our household over the years. Everything from kittens and puppies to guinea pigs, parakeets, and even a pet rat made their home with us at one time or another. Mom was usually very patient with my furry and feathered friends.

*Fluffy the bunny rabbit; courtesy Fahad Puthawala /
pexels.com*

At one point, we had a pet rabbit. I can't recall the details as to how he came to live with us, but he was quite messy and definitely not Mom's favorite. One day, I came home from school, and he was gone! Somehow, he had gotten out of his cage. I was very distraught that my bunny had come up missing.

About an hour later, there was a knock on the door. Mom opened it to see some kids who lived on our block, looking up at her with big smiles.

"We found Nancy's bunny!" They chorused, one of them holding my slightly bedraggled pet in their arms.

Mom forced a smile. "Why, that's great! Thank you!" She managed as I burst past her to reclaim my furry friend.

"Thank you!" I gasped as I snuggled him next to my cheek.

Years later, I found out that Mom, not happy with the perpetual mess that accompanied my rabbit's cage—and unbeknownst to me—had taken Fluffy out to the fields behind Terrace Elementary and set him free. She figured he would be happy out there and find other bunnies to play with. She had not counted on our neighborhood kids finding him and returning him to me!

Life on Rorary Drive

Eddie blowing out birthday candles at the dining room
table, with a view of the kitchen; author photo

I t was certainly a different time, growing up in the '70s. We usually woke up to a rooster crowing and a full day of either school, sports, scouts, or play, depending on the time of year. Eddie and I had daily chores. One of us would set the table for dinner, pulling napkins out of the napkin holder

Mom kept in the center of the dining room table and placing the silverware we needed for the meal on them—four places. Afterwards, the other one would clear the table and wipe it with a sponge. Whoever set the table also got the carpet sweeper out of the hall closet and pushed it around the dining area.

The kitchen on Rorary Drive; author photo

We would both meet in the kitchen to wash and dry the dishes. Eddie usually stood on the left side of the double sink and filled it with soapy water. He would swirl the dishes around in it while wiping them off with a sponge. I was stationed next to him on the right side to rinse off the dishes he handed me and place them in the dish rack to drain. We would take turns drying the dishes.

In the early evening during the summer, we could hear the locusts trilling. The neighborhood kids would run out of their houses to play while the grownups meandered up and down the sidewalk, pausing in driveways to chat with the neighbors. A sweet older couple lived across the street and two doors over. The husband, with his twinkly blue eyes and white hair, would be out front in his overalls. If anyone needed some grandfatherly wisdom, they sought him out.

Everyone knew everyone else. Further down our side of the

street, the father of a family of four might be welding in his garage, the door up and his familiar welding mask in place, with sparks flying. He would see me on the sidewalk and greet me, jokingly saying, "Well, hello, George!" I always thought that was very funny. When I was in elementary school, I interviewed him on what it was like to be an engineer. He was working at Texas Instruments when the transistor was invented, and he told me they had no idea what an important innovation that was at the time. He inspired me to think about becoming an engineer.

*Eddie and Nancy on their bicycles, getting ready to ride
to Terrace Swimming Pool; author photo*

His daughter took on the task of teaching me how to ride a bicycle. I had an old red, slightly rusty bicycle, and my heart started racing when my mom took off the training wheels. Our neighbor's daughter ran alongside me, up and down the sidewalk, helping me balance, until she could see I was able to balance for myself and let go. I was so happy I could ride! Mom and Dad eventually bought me a purple Schwinn bike with a white and purple basket. Eddie's was a bronze color. We spent all summer riding our bikes and going swimming!

We would often go across the street and four houses down because a brother and sister had a basketball hoop in their driveway. We would play touch football in the street and never had to worry about cars going too fast. We had a big pile of leaves that had fallen from the huge tree in our front yard, and we had a lot of fun jumping into that leaf pile. We would play hide and seek up and down the street once it started to get dark and the fireflies (we also called them lightning bugs) were out.

Another favorite activity was chasing those lightning bugs on warm summer nights. Mom gave me a mason jar with holes in the lid to put them in. I could see their lights glowing on and off in our front yard and would manage to catch a few, but I always turned them loose when it was time to go back inside.

I had a bow and arrow set and would often shoot my bow at a target I put on the metal shed in our backyard—not realizing I was creating dozens of puncture marks in the metal until my Dad noticed and had me move the target. I moved it to the fence between our house and the neighbor's—no more puncture marks. I had a similar fiasco with my string art kit on the kitchen table (and the reason Mom had to start keeping a tablecloth on it), but that's another story...

Nancy's porch view; author photo

The view from our front porch was wonderful. Looking through the various rectangular parts of the lattice woodwork was like looking at life from different perspectives. I would sit in the middle of the big square, dangling my skinny legs while reading a book, and dreaming of adventures.

Growing Up with Eddie

Easy way to climb onto the roof from the porch; author photo

I spent hours climbing those wooden beams, which also enabled me to easily scramble onto the roof and observe the comings and goings of our neighborhood.

Eddie and Nancy on the tire swing in the front yard; author photo

Or I would climb the huge tree in the front yard all the way to the top—I could see all over Richardson! I climbed it at night once and didn't want to climb down; the bright lights that I could see in the dark sky from that heavenly view amazed me.

To climb it, I had to jump up, grab the limb closest to the ground with both hands and swing myself up, then use hand and footholds to make my way to the top, which towered over our house. That same limb also held a rope to a tire that Eddie and I spent many hours swinging on.

Rainy days were spent playing games and cards. When we were younger, Checkers, Old Maid, and Go Fish were staples. When we got older, Eddie and I would play Black Jack or get two decks and combine them for a game of War. Sometimes in the evening, Mom and Dad would join us for a game of Monopoly, Scrabble, or Yahtzee.

Growing up, we often didn't have a lot of money, but my mom gave me a wonderful gift that surpasses any of the toys we couldn't afford—she gave me the gift of a love for reading. Every night, she would sit by my bed with me and Eddie, and read to us from Babar the Elephant. She took us on exciting voyages with her words and nurtured in us a love for books.

Starting in third grade, I couldn't wait to get my report card because if I got all As and Bs, I could count on Mom taking me to Kmart to pick out a Nancy Drew mystery. I can picture the racks of books in my mind. While Mom did her shopping, I would go through each one on the display until I settled on my next quest. If there were horses involved, that book went to the top of my list.

Shopping at Kmart was always a treat. The "Blue Light Special" announcement would send us all running to where we could see the rotating blue light flashing. Kmart also offered "Layaway," a blessing for many families, especially when Christmas shopping.

Evenings were spent in the living room with my family. We each had our "spot," and mine was the green chair next to the lamp stand. I would sit cuddled up and reading while Mom, Dad, and Eddie watched TV.

When bedtime arrived, I would say my goodnights, and I couldn't wait to get to bed. Hiding under my blanket with my flashlight, I was transported to other worlds. My stack of library books was a free ticket to wondrous adventures. I would keep half an ear listening for Mom's footsteps, so I could shut off my flashlight before she saw me. Looking back, I am quite sure she knew I was reading and smiled as she checked on me while I did my best imitation of being asleep.

Whenever I got out of bed in the wintertime, the cold hardwood floor on my bare feet would jolt me awake. Speaking of bare feet, that is how we spent much of our summer. Our feet became toughened, and we easily walked on the ordinary cement of sidewalks and alleys, but we did hop and dance across black asphalt roads on a hot day.

There always seemed to be a home improvement project in the works. Back then, family members were called upon to provide the labor. An important improvement that was implemented almost immediately when we moved in, was moving the light switch to the hall bathroom, from the shower to the hallway. While it was a bit odd turning on the bathroom light before entering—it was much safer! Janet's husband was an electrician and took care of that for us.

Over the years, we removed our chain link fence and replaced it with a wooden one (I mainly helped with painting it —a dark red), Dad wallpapered the kitchen, hallway, living, and dining rooms, and Eddie and his best friend replaced the laminated tile in the kitchen with new ones—they did a great job and we were very proud of them.

Schwinns, Snowmen, and Thunderstorms

Nancy's first bicycle, with Mom and Eddie; author photo

Nancy Golden

Eddie's first bicycle, with Dad; author photo

Bicycles were our main source of transportation and entertainment. We rode them to school and in the summer, all around our neighborhoods. We built ramps out of scrap wood and dared each other to ride up them and soar into the air. We taught ourselves how to do pop wheelies and ride with no hands. We would haul a buddy on our handlebars or behind us if they needed a ride. We put a card in the spokes with a clothespin to make it sound like a motorcycle. It gave us a sense of independence at a young age. We didn't have to wait for someone to give us a ride somewhere. Having a bicycle was a ticket to freedom—roaming our town with our friends.

*Dad and Nancy posing with Frosty - the Cowboy
Snowman; author photo*

*Mom and Nancy posing with Frosty - the Cowboy
Snowman; author photo*

Building a snowman was a rare and very happy occurrence growing up. Richardson, Texas, is not known for its snowfall, and so when we did get enough accumulation of the cold white stuff, we headed out to build our version of Frosty.

*Nancy with the snowman she helped build, in front of
the Richardson Fire Station; author photo*

We built a snowman in front of the Richardson Fire Station
during the winter of 1978.

Neapolitan ice cream; author photo

Mom usually bought Neapolitan ice cream (chocolate,

vanilla, and strawberry in the same carton). I always scooped out chocolate, and Eddie always wanted strawberry. When our first choice was gone, we would dig into the vanilla, so the inside of the carton looked pretty funny as we dug our way through it.

Mom was very clever; she would let us have ice cream during thunderstorms. Instead of being afraid, we associated stormy weather with ice cream.

Richardson Daily News Paper Route

*Stack of Richardson Daily News papers, ready to be rolled,
on the living room floor; author photo*

E ddie and I shared a paper route when we were in
elementary school. The Richardson Daily News
would come by our house and leave a stack of papers
on our porch, bound by a clear, thin plastic strap. We would
grab the strap and haul the papers inside. A large box of rubber
bands, a huge ink-stained grey cloth bag to hold the papers, a

pair of scissors to cut the plastic strap, and a beat-up clip board that had a piece of notebook paper taped to it (with street names and numbers listed in columns) completed our supplies.

We would sit in the middle of our living room, grabbing one paper off the stack at a time and rolling it, then securing it with a rubber band, repeating this process until all of the papers were rolled. We would then stuff the cloth bag with the papers and take turns throwing them. The bag went over our shoulder, and the clipboard was clamped to the handlebars of our bicycle. If a house number had an asterisk next to it, that meant we had to make sure we threw the paper so that it landed on the porch. We got pretty good at it, but sometimes we would miss and have to get off our bicycle, pick it up, and toss it onto the porch.

After riding the route for a while, we no longer needed the clipboard—we had the houses memorized. It was a pretty tough route because some of the streets were named Edgehill, Hillside, Hillcrest, and Hilltop—they were pretty steep. If the weather was bad, Mom would pop the trunk of her Cutlass Supreme, and we would sit in the trunk with the newspapers stacked next to us and throw the papers from her car as she drove up and down the streets.

Back then, the paper boy or girl was responsible for collecting the subscription money from each paper customer. That meant going out in the evening when people were more likely to be home from work, knocking on doors, and requesting their monthly payment. In the winter, we would be bundled up, and it would always be dark when it was time to start collecting.

Knock, Knock

The door would open, and sometimes I would be invited inside, and offered a treat while my customer dug for some bills and change or wrote a check to the Richardson Daily News. Other times, I was left on the doorstep as they went in search of their payment. About 50% of the customers would include a tip. Somehow, it was a more trusting time. Back then, I was never fearful tromping the streets of our neighborhood at night, carrying what was obviously a bank bag that I put the payments in.

I also got to glimpse how other people lived. In the apartments on La Salle, one of my customers requested their paper always porched, which meant getting off my bike, going up some steps, and opening a door to the entrance of the building that housed four apartments, two on the bottom floor, and two on the second floor. There were a couple of these units side by side on the other side of La Salle between Royal Crest and Apollo.

Older lady in wheelchair; courtesy Davis Arenas /
pexels.com

I remember feeling very awkward the first time the apartment's occupant came to the door. She was an older lady in a wheelchair, and her chihuahua charged me, barking. She got Poncho calmed down and cheerfully found her purse and paid me. That was a defining moment for me. I had never met someone in a wheelchair before, and I was amazed that she lived there and took care of herself. I never again grumbled about having to get off my bicycle to put her paper in front of her door.

I loved collecting at Christmas time because that is when most people were friendly and had a tip for me. The houses were typically decorated with Christmas lights and decorations, if not on the outside, I usually saw some evidence of Christmas when they opened their doors. Most houses had a festively decorated Christmas tree.

But I remember one house didn't have any decorations, and as I stood there waiting for their payment, I felt sad for the kids living there. Perhaps I didn't need to, I recalled the menorah Mom set out this time of year in celebration of Hanukkah. Having grown up in an Italian-Jewish household, I understood that different cultures had their own celebrations, but I felt very blessed that we celebrated Christmas. I wondered about who lived there and what their holiday traditions were.

Sibling Squabbles

Eddie and I were very close growing up, but we often squabbled as siblings are bound to do. When you first entered our house, you would find yourself in the living room. A hallway leading to the bedrooms was centered across from the recliner that was reserved for our dad. A couch resided under the front window, and a chair with a lamp was to one side of the hall entryway.

If you entered the hall, a bathroom was immediately on the left side of the hallway. A hall closet was on the right, a few feet further down, and at the end of the hall was the door to my bedroom. Taking a right at the end of the hall takes you past Eddie's bedroom and into the kitchen.

You could walk through the kitchen, enter the dining area (which also had an opening at the far side, with steps that led down to our garage that had been converted to a den), turn right, and find yourself back in the living room. This arrangement made it possible for a child to race through the house in a somewhat circular pattern.

One of my favorite things to do was to make my big brother mad, as is often the case with little sisters. Because of the house's circular pattern, I could aggravate my brother bad enough that he would start chasing me. I was faster than him (probably because I was highly motivated to escape), and would run through the house and duck into the bathroom, locking the door behind me with a push and twist on the doorknob just before he got close enough to open it. Inside the bathroom was a cupboard with shelves across from the bathtub, near the door. I always kept a good book on one of the shelves in case Eddie was persistent and I would be stuck there a while until he cooled off and left.

One time, Eddie didn't cool off but instead, kept slamming into the bathroom door. I must have really made him mad about something! Suddenly, we heard a CRACKKKKK and the top of the door fell forward, towards me. We immediately called a truce to evaluate the situation. The wood where the top hinge was screwed into the door frame had cracked and was hanging outward, no longer supporting the top part of the door.

We agreed to extend the truce and decided the best thing to do would be to join forces and pool our allowance, run to M.E. Moses (the local Five & Dime), and buy a can of wood putty and paint so we could repair the damage before Mom and Dad came home. We managed to complete the task before our parents arrived, and they were never the wiser. Eddie and I didn't always get along, but we always had each other's backs, and in this case, it was also a case of mutual self-preservation at stake.

~

Growing Up with Eddie

Eddie on our couch with his foot in a cast; author photo

One time, Eddie broke his foot, and his foot and lower leg were in a cast. The throwing portion of the paper route fell to me, but he would still help roll the papers. One day, I managed to get him really mad (yet again). He was very easy to outrun since he had the cast on, but that didn't stop him. He was blocking my usual route to dive into the hall bathroom, and the only way to escape him was out the front door, down the porch steps, pell-mell across the yard, and down the sidewalk.

But that didn't stop my big brother. He scooped up an armful of rolled papers and, hopping on one foot, made his way down the porch steps and across the driveway, throwing papers in my direction as he continued to hop. I don't remember what I did to make him so mad, but I have a picture frozen in time in my mind of him hopping down the sidewalk with his cast, throwing those papers at me.

Whenever Eddie and I started squabbling and Dad was around, he would make us come together and "kiss and make up." As soon as we gave each other the obligatory kiss on the cheek, we would both start rubbing our cheeks to rub away the kiss. Dad would just laugh at the two of us and say, "You're just rubbing it in."

Baseball at Terrace Park

Eddie in his baseball uniform; author photo

I remember so many summer nights at Terrace Park watching Eddie play baseball—he was the catcher.

Terrace Park baseball field; author photo

Let me close my eyes and describe the sights and sounds of an evening baseball game:

Terrace Park had a baseball field with bleachers. A concession stand was easily accessible, providing snow cones, cotton candy, foot-long bubble gum, sour cherries, bottle caps, and extra-wide taffy. Mom, Dad, and I would climb the wooden bleachers and make sure there were no splinters before sitting down. I would wriggle with anticipation at the one treat I was allowed to have every game. I decided on a suicide snow cone. Back then, no one we knew contemplated suicide or associated the snow cone with the actual heartbreaking act—it was just the name given to a snow cone that consisted of short spurts of every flavor available in a strange concoction that was popular with kids at the time, meant to show the person eating it was daring enough to risk death (but not really).

It was dusk, and the bugs were out in force. The baseball players would come out onto the field, and all that separated us from them was a tall chain link fence. We always had a good view of my brother since home plate was right on the other side of it. The bleachers would fill with parents and kids, and as the game progressed, we would play tag around the bleachers in between innings. "Batta, batta, batta, come on, batta" would pierce the night air, and we would all hold our breath when a foul pop fly soared upward, until more times than not, my brother managed to catch it.

Night fell as the game progressed, and there was something very special about being outdoors under the canopy of stars, watching the game illuminated by the lights that came on when the sky darkened. Parents would cheer, and red dirt would fly. As the night progressed, I would get sleepy and, sitting next to my parents, try to stay awake. Finally, the game would end, and we would gather around my brother, congratulating him on his play. The team would swarm the concession stand to get their well-earned treats, and then we would pile into the car for the short drive home.

Family Fishing

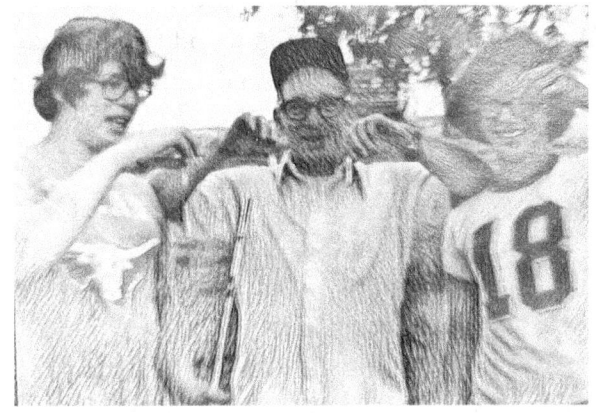

Eddie, Dad, and Nancy showing off their minnows;
author photo

Eddie fishing with a bamboo pole; author photo

We loved to go fishing, and there were plenty of opportunities in and around Richardson. We had bamboo poles for simple fishing poles, or we used a rod and reel.

Dad carrying an ice chest for a picnic; author photo

Fishing usually meant we were also going on a picnic. Mom

would pack a cooler with food and drinks for Dad to carry to a likely picnic place.

Father and son time; author photo

Eddie and Nancy, ready to find a fishing spot; author photo

Eddie and Dad showing off their catch; author photo

So many wonderful memories of fun family time being outdoors together!

Halloween in our Neighborhood

Eddie and Nancy in Halloween costumes; author photo

Halloween was light-hearted and fun when we were growing up, filled with kids wearing hard plastic masks ranging from superheroes to Snoopy, or creative homemade costumes, usually carrying pillow cases for treat bags. Yard decorations leaned more toward pumpkins and cats, although the occasional ghost, skeleton, or cackling witch stirring her cauldron (played by the homeowner in costume) would add an element of scary fun. No graphic displays or disturbing images could be found and would not have been tolerated. It was a sweeter, simpler time.

Our first Halloween in our neighborhood on Rorary Drive was rather humorous. Where we used to live (we moved to Texas from New York in the late '60s), young trick-or-treaters started their Halloween adventure before it got dark, so Mom had us ready to go and we started knocking on doors when it was still daylight. Imagine our surprise when we were politely but firmly told it wasn't time yet—and to come back after dark. We went back home where Eddie and I anxiously waited for the sun to go down. Finally, it was time! And the following year, we knew what to do.

My mom was a wonderful, caring woman. She had such an amazing sense of community and volunteerism. She loved holidays and always tried to make them special for everyone around her. One year, when we were still too young to trick-or-treat by ourselves, Mom wanted to do her part in providing Halloween fun for the neighborhood kids. Her solution was to have treats on our porch while we were walking the neighborhood.

I'll never forget the care Mom put into making those treat bags for that Halloween. She bought small white paper bags with a Halloween graphic on one side. She also bought candy and small plastic toys (like you would find in a cereal box). She carefully filled each bag with treats and twisted the top of each bag shut. She had found a large, shallow, cardboard box and carefully placed them in the box and left it on our porch on a bench by the door, with the porch light on. She took a piece of paper and wrote "Take One" and taped it to the front of our door, visible to any trick-or-treaters coming onto our porch for a treat.

Eddie and I eagerly waited for her to finish, in our costumes and holding bags to collect candy from our neighbors. Mom was finally ready, and it had gotten dark, so we started down our street, going to each house. Our costumes were much simpler back then and not too scary. We either made them ourselves or picked them out at Kmart. I can't remember what we wore, but I do remember going from house to house while Mom waited for us on the sidewalk.

We started across the street from our house and made our way around the block. One house gave out full-sized candy bars, and another gave out caramel apples! We felt like we had struck the jackpot! Mom decided we should come back toward our street and make our way up the other side.

Walking down the sidewalk, we peered at the bench and, much to our dismay—all of the bags were already gone! Some rascals took more than their fair share and left nothing for anyone else. Mom was so disappointed, and even at that young age, I felt sorry for her. She had tried to do a nice thing, and it had not worked out as she planned.

But it never stopped her from trying. The following year, she didn't leave treat bags out. Instead, Mom took us trick-or-treating while Dad stayed home and when kids came to the door, he handed out the candy she had ready for them.

Sports

*Baby sister Nancy gazing adoringly at big brother Eddie
in his R.S.I. football uniform; author photo*

Eddie on the Terrace Vikings soccer team; author photo

Over the years, Eddie and I played on various R.S. I. and school teams. Eddie played baseball, football, and soccer. He was very dedicated to his teams, and his coaches had a powerful impact on his life. He told a story once when asked if he was going to persevere or give up. He said his football coaches had taught him to "gut it out" when things got hard. To keep going and not give up. That is how Eddie lived his life. Once he decided to do something, no matter how hard it got, he never gave up.

Growing Up with Eddie

Nancy in her Blue Racers soccer uniform; author photo

I played soccer for the Blue Racers, in elementary and junior high school, and I was pretty good. Our coaches worked hard to support us and we all knew each other. We usually practiced at Terrace Park, and our team always did well, including winning a championship.

I tried out for the North Texas All-Stars and made the team. We practiced hard to get ready for the North Texas Championship Tournament. Eddie was a waiter at Kip's Big Boy at the time, an iconic local restaurant with the huge Big Boy statue out front. His manager told him that he couldn't get off work to watch me in the tournament, so he quit. He wasn't going to miss watching his baby sister play. The tournament ran all weekend, and we won the championship.

I also played softball and basketball. I was on a basketball team that practiced at a school off of Arapaho Road near Waterview Drive. I don't know if I liked the adventure of being on a team that was not in my immediate neighborhood more (although still in Richardson), or the fact that we passed Baskin-

Robbins on the way to practice, since there was always a good chance Mom would stop on the way home and get us each a Jamocha Almond Fudge ice cream cone.

I remember one time we got our ice creams to go and I bit into mine as Mom was driving us home. There was a strange-looking object sticking out of it. At first, I thought it was a nut but on closer investigation, I determined it was a June bug! I was really glad they had handed me that cone and my mom the other one. Since she was driving, she probably wouldn't have noticed and eaten it!

Sports had a huge role in both of our lives and I am grateful for all of the love and support Mom and Dad poured into our athletic endeavors; they paid for the privilege we enjoyed of being on those teams, they drove us to practice, and encouraged us to practice at home. They came to all of our games and cheered for us.

Mom and Eddie at a football game; author photo

Dad and Eddie at a football game; author photo

*Nancy wearing her All-Stars soccer shirt with Mom, in the
front yard; author photo*

Participating in sports taught us not only about team work,
but also about setting goals and persevering even when it gets
really hard. I am especially grateful that Eddie and I got to
experience that part of growing up in Richardson.

Television Shows

Television in the living room on Rorary Drive; author photo

I think watching television in the '70s was much more balanced than today; probably because we only had Channels 4, 5, 8, 11, 13, 21, and 39. I would race home from Terrace Elementary so I could watch my favorite "horse" show: Fury, which was about a wild black stallion and the boy

Joey, who saved his life. I loved following their adventures on the Broken Wheel Ranch.

Mom and Dad were usually at work when I got home. Being a latchkey kid (I wore a thick green yarn necklace with my house key attached to it, around my neck and tucked inside my shirt for safekeeping) had its advantages since I could watch television before doing my homework, with no one the wiser. I also watched the Mickey Mouse Club reruns of the serial, Spin and Marty, because of the western theme. Both shows were in black and white and captivated me. Other shows that provided after-school entertainment included Gilligan's Island, I Dream of Jeannie, The Brady Bunch, and The Partridge Family.

Hogan's Heroes was our Dad's favorite television show, and sometimes we would get to eat on TV trays when Dad came home from work and wanted to watch it.

Eddie and I would get up early on Saturday mornings to watch cartoons in our pajamas, eating our bowls of cereal sitting cross-legged in front of the TV. Eddie's favorite was The Roadrunner Show, and of course, Bugs Bunny, Tom and Jerry, Yogi Bear, The Mighty Heroes (Remember Diaper Man?!), Speed Racer, and The Flintstones were all staples on our viewing list.

Growing Up with Eddie

Living room on Rorary Drive; author photo

Sunday evenings, our whole family would sit in the living room for the Wonderful World of Disney. Since it was only an hour, we usually had to watch a movie in two parts, waiting a whole week to finish it. We each had our "spot" in the living room: Dad in his recliner, Mom and Eddie on the couch in front of the living room window, and my green stuffed chair next to the hallway with a light stand next to it so I could curl up and read.

When we were allowed to stay up late, nighttime television included M*A*S*H, Mary Tyler Moore, The Carol Burnett Show, The Honeymooners, and The Tonight Show with Johnny Carson. Of course, at ten o'clock we would see the "It's ten o'clock, do you know where your children are?" onscreen, and at midnight, the station would stop transmitting shows and simply show a test pattern (sometimes after showing an American flag and playing patriotic music).

❧

One show we watched could make me a little anxious. Back then, television was seldom graphic; our imaginations could make things much scarier than reality. So imagine this:

The character in Twilight Zone finds himself unexpectedly walking through walls, into another dimension. You are sitting with your family, eyes wide, as the story unfolds. The show runs to completion with the typical signature ending, Rod Serling's voice, "In The Twilight Zone..."

That night, I entered my bedroom and looked around warily. I shut the light and crawled into bed, somewhat nervous. My bed was against two walls, one alongside and one at the head of it. I placed my hands on the wall and pushed, then continued to move my hands along the length of both walls, reassuring myself that they were stable and I wouldn't fall through them and into another dimension like the man on The Twilight Zone. After that episode, I did that nightly for a couple of weeks.

Music and Mood Rings

E ddie and I enjoyed technology during the early '70s in the form of our Porta-fi speakers. We each had one in our bedroom, and the stereo console in the den could transmit music to the Porta-fis—they were essentially wireless speakers. You turned the knob on the front to turn it on and set the volume. The only downside was that you had to go across the house to change the music. The wireless aspect was a very big deal at the time. Mom loved music, and we enjoyed that stereo for many years.

Eddie's room was right next to mine, and I would often hear "Yellow Submarine" or "Sgt. Pepper's Lonely Hearts Club Band" playing—he loved The Beatles! We both enjoyed listening to music, and we would take our paper route money and buy our favorite 45s. While my taste leaned toward the Osmond Brothers (I was in love with Donny Osmond), Eddie would come home with "Billy, Don't Be a Hero," "I Don't Like Spiders and Snakes," "The Battle of New Orleans," in addition to anything Beatles. I also had my own portable record player so I could play records in my room. I wore that thing out playing "Puppy Love" and "Crazy Horses." My taste in music evolved, and I moved on from "Puppy Love" to "Just the Way You Are" by Billy Joel. One of my favorite albums was "The Stranger," and since Eddie also liked The Piano Man's music, we played it often.

Eddie and I both contributed to our collection of 45s, and as young adults, we developed a tradition. Why we kept them in a crinkled-up brown grocery bag, I'll never know, but we did —instead of something more sensible. Every year or so, we would trade our collection (in that brown paper bag) back and forth. I miss that...

~

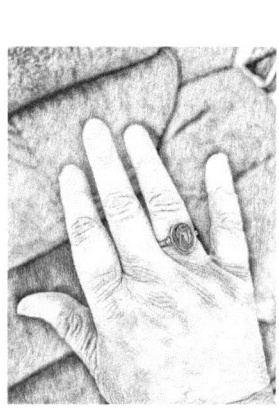

Nancy's mood ring; author photo

When mood rings first came out, I saved up my allowance to get one and wore mine all the time. An opalescent ring that would change color with my mood—so cool! My pet rock lived on a shelf in my bedroom, my clackers were ready to bang together when I was bored (the balls were a green-swirly color), I used Silly Putty to make fun impressions of the Sunday comics, and a yo-yo was always handy on a rainy day to practice "walk the dog." Essentials for a kid in the '70s!

Dallas Continental Inn

Daddy/Daughter date; author photo

I was probably about nine years old when Mom told me Daddy was taking me on a date! She told me to dress in my Sunday best. I was both excited and nervous—where were we going? I walked out into our living room, and there was my big, strong, handsome daddy, wearing a suit and tie.

Mom was standing off to the side, beaming. I ran to my daddy, and he enveloped me in a bear hug.

"Are you ready?"

"Yes!" I smiled up at him. "Where are we going?"

"You'll see," he winked at Mom.

We got into his car, and I got to sit in the front seat. We didn't have far to go, the Continental Inn was right off of Central Expressway near Spring Valley. Back then, it was considered an elite hotel, boasting 150 deluxe rooms, 4 stalls for horses (this horse-crazy little girl thought that was amazing!), a swimming pool, meeting and banquet rooms, and a high-end restaurant. Our destination was the restaurant.

In order to fully appreciate the magnitude of this experience, I should share that we rarely ate out. Dad worked for himself, and it was very difficult starting and running a business, with no money for extras, at least in the beginning. This was a very special event that my parents had put money aside for.

We got out of the car, and I clutched my dad's arm as we walked through the parking lot and into the restaurant. We followed the host to our table, and he held out my seat for me. Daddy said I could order anything I wanted. I don't remember the food at all, but I do remember how special I felt.

Sun Rexall and Texas Blue Law

*Sun Rexall Drugs, "The Old Country Store," 41
Richardson Heights Shopping Center in Richardson;
courtesy Nanci Kaplan Duplant*

"I can see the Sun!" We would shout excitedly when my dad aimed our car toward Sun Rexall, the iconic drug store that served the Richardson community along with JC Penney, Wyatt's Cafeteria, White's Automotive, and Dad & Lad's in Heights Shopping Center. The sign was a Richardson landmark with a revolving clock that stood 70 feet high.

At Sun Rexall, you could find everything under the sun, including a mynah bird named Jo-Jo to provide entertainment and a soda fountain to get a frosty treat or hot fudge sundae. I remember when handheld electronic calculators first came out —Sun Rexall had them in a case on display. We were amazed that the numbers would light up red!!

Texas Blue Law affected Sunday shopping; author design

The only shopping we typically did on Sundays was to stop at 7-11 for Slurpees after Mass. Once, we went to Sun Rexall on a Sunday only to find we had to come back the next day. Since the Blue Law was in effect, our buying power was limited —when we got to the cash register, Dad had to put back the frying pan he wanted to buy.

If you would like to learn more about Sun Rexall Drugs, there is a wonderful book that details its history—*Mr. Sun Rexall Drug: One Family's Lasting Legacy in Pharmaceuticals*

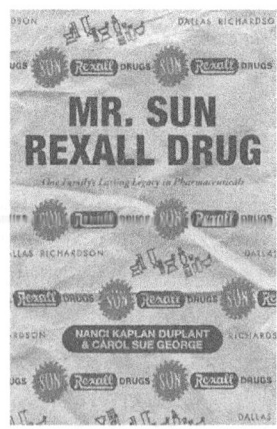

Fire in the Bathtub

When we first moved to our house on Rorary, we had a wonderful next-door neighbor. If you read *Cowboy Boots and Weights,* you'll see a picture of the Christmas stockings she handmade for me and Eddie.

I was a very sensitive child, and I found it very difficult to lie. If I tried, my face would turn red, and my hands would tremble. I would feel terrible and eventually blurt out the truth. Just knowing my parents were upset with me was enough punishment.

Eddie, on the other hand, had no problem fabricating a story to cover his tracks. Our neighbor was a very smart lady and could see right through any falsehood my brother would attempt, to get out of trouble. She loved him, but she also knew he could be a mischievous scamp.

While not the actual fire, Eddie is in the actual bathtub;
author photo

One day, after school, Mom was at work when Eddie found some matches and decided it would be fun to start a fire in the bathtub. He figured that would be the ideal place since he could put it out if he needed to. The newspaper started burning faster than Eddie thought, and soon the house filled with smoke. I ran next door to get help, and fortunately, our neighbor was home and came over.

She helped us douse the fire, and when Eddie came up with a lame excuse about a science homework assignment, she wasn't buying it. She set Mom straight when Eddie told her his story, and a call to the school confirmed our neighbor's analysis of the situation.

Heat for the Seat wooden paddle; author photo

We had a paddle with the words "Heat for the Seat" printed on it, hanging in our kitchen. While I never needed it applied, Eddie occasionally felt its sting. When Dad came home that evening, that day was one of those times.

Babar

Nancy eagerly waiting for Mom to read a bedtime story;
author photo

"Eddie, get in here," Mom called out, sitting in the orange plastic chair she had moved closer to my bed. I sat with the covers pulled back, anxiously waiting for my brother to make an appearance. I was in first grade, and it was my favorite time of night, about twenty minutes before our bedtime.

"I'm brushing my teeth," came Eddie's garbled reply from down the hall.

"Hurry up," I yelled before Mom could respond. "I want to hear Mom read!"

Bedtime reading: Babar; author photo

Mom looked at me and smiled. She waited patiently, holding one of my favorite books, Babar the King. The human qualities the author attached to the elephants and their world-wide adventures were very exciting to me.

Eddie finally burst into my bedroom and dove onto my bed, flipped over, sat up, and grinned.

"I'm ready!"

Mom eyed my unruly brother for a moment and shook her head slightly with a smile tugging at her mouth, then opened the pages and began to read.

I am very grateful for our mom's desire to instill in us not just a love of reading, but a thirst for stories that would take us on adventures and stir our imaginations. Those early days of my childhood were precious as Mom gave us her love and attention through our bedtime stories. Reading transports us away from our troubles for a while, it inspires us, it teaches us... It is a precious gift.

After our latest adventure, Mom would close the book and shoo Eddie out of bed. Amidst "Love you's" and hugs, my bedtime was peaceful, and tired after my busy day, I would curl up with my favorite stuffed animal and fall asleep.

Butterflies, Honeysuckles, and Pong

We were expected to play outside unless it was pouring rain and we became really good at finding things to do in our immediate neighborhood. Interestingly enough, brownish grey butterflies seemed to inhabit most of the trees on our block. They would often land on a tree trunk and sit with their wings folded together. After watching one of the other kids stealthily approach a tree and carefully but swiftly reach forward with two fingers and grasp a butterfly by its wings, I attempted to do so. It took me a few tries. The goal was not to keep it, but to be successful in catching it, then immediately turning it loose. When I found out that touching a butterfly's wings could damage them, I quit catching them. Preying mantises, grasshoppers, locusts, geckos, frogs, and doodle bugs were all fair game in our pursuit of observing our natural surroundings.

Honeysuckles grew on vines in our neighborhood and a sweet childhood delight was to tear off a flower and while holding it, pull down on the stem at the bottom. Once the stem was nearly out, a drop of nectar would appear at the flower's base, ready to slurp and enjoy.

On rainy days, we would play indoor games, mostly Monopoly, cards, or checkers. We were the first on our block to get a Pong game, and that was absolutely amazing. By today's standards, the simple black screen with white paddles, ball, and numbers keeping score may be boring, but to us, it was astounding. Being able to move paddles up and down to play a game of ping pong on our television set was mind-boggling.

Mom had already instilled a love for playing ping pong in me at the Rec Center, so it was a lot of fun to transition that to an electronic game. Eddie and I soon got pretty good at it. One of my favorite things to do was to position the paddles just right so that the game would play itself, hitting the ball back and forth for as long as we left it on.

In later years, reminiscent of the Pong play of our childhood, I was a participant in a software bootcamp, and for my final project, I decided to recreate Pong with a couple of extra "features." I included the option for team play and inputting the names of the players along with a very special option: I challenged my instructor to a game and when he entered his first name, the paddle became very small (I had included code for when he input the specific letters of his name, it would reduce the size of the paddle), and when I entered my first name, the paddle became very large (again, additional code for my name).

Fortunately, my instructor had a good sense of humor and appreciated the extra coding it took to do that. We were doing our project presentations with many of the upper managers of the company watching in order to consider us for employment. Thanks to my childhood Pong—I got the job!

Horse Play

D ad was an entrepreneur, and he always wanted to be a cowboy. When Eddie and I were growing up, he started his own business, which he and my mom ran out of our house. Before the garage became our den, it was the office of R & L Sales.

Nancy with Dad in front of his baby blue Cadillac,
advertising R&L Sales on the door; author photo

He sold home security products, including burglar alarms and yard lights. While we were poor for some of my childhood, we had a good run when his business took off, before the energy crisis.

Dad would wear a cowboy hat, western shirt, and cowboy boots. I gave him a western bolo for Christmas. He bought a used baby blue Cadillac with a white top and had signs on the front doors advertising R & L Sales. He loved being a Texan. When he came home from work at night, I would pull his boots off for him.

I was a horse-crazy little girl, and instead of Barbie dolls, I played with my Breyer horse models. I was still in elementary school when, one day, something beyond my wildest dreams occurred. Mom and Dad announced that we were going to buy a horse. Dad bought a beautiful bay mare from someone he knew through his business. Her name was Cindy. Thus began an idyllic two years spent at the various barns we kept her at. So many adventures!!

Nancy on Cindy; author photo

I remember one place where we stabled Cindy, they had peacocks roaming the grounds. The area was forested and had a creek running through it. I made friends with an Irish Setter who would show up when I was getting ready for a ride. I would grab an empty feed bucket and tie a rope to the handle, then scramble up on Cindy's back, clutching the rope so that I could bring the bucket with me. I rode out alone and rarely rode with a saddle, usually in shorts and a t-shirt and tennis shoes—my skinny legs hanging down Cindy's back, slick in the summer since she had shed her winter coat. I could grab a handful of her thick black mane if we were scrambling up a hill, so I didn't slide off.

I would ride Cindy to the edge of the creek's embankment and jump off of her. She would stand, waiting patiently, the Irish Setter watching nearby. The sides were steep, and from the top, I would lower the bucket until it fell into the creek. As it became engulfed with water, it would fall over on its side, the perfect hiding place for unsuspecting fish. I would tie the end of the rope to a branch, find a log to stand on, and scramble back up onto Cindy's back. Wandering through the trees with Red following, loping through the patches of open fields, I would eventually make my way back to where I had tied the rope.

Fishing with a bucket; courtesy Wikimedia Commons / U.S. Fish and Wildlife Service - Public Domain

Sliding off Cindy's back again, I would grab the end of the rope and pull up the bucket as fast as I could. Heavy with water sloshing out the sides, I managed to bring it up over the edge. Grabbing the handle, I would back away from the embankment and peer into the bucket to see what I might have caught. Inevitably, a sunfish or two would be swimming frantically around, having thought the bucket was a convenient cave to hide from predators. Depending on my mood, the fish either went for a high dive back into the creek, or I left them in the bucket and carried it back to the barn, where they became dinner for the barn cats.

When I first started riding Cindy, she had an unfortunate habit of bolting (meaning running away at a high rate of speed). Usually, when this happens, an experienced rider will turn the horse, causing her to run in a circle, which controls the direction the horse is running and also tires the horse out so that the rider can regain control. But being a skinny kid, my arms were not strong enough to turn Cindy.

One day, I was riding in a saddle and I was alone, when Cindy bolted. Since I wasn't strong enough to circle her and I knew that she was headed directly for a fence, my mind whirred, trying to decide what to do. I didn't know what she would do, and I was afraid she would slam into the fence at the high rate of speed she was going. We had been riding in a field next to a cement-paved road when she started her headlong gallop, and we veered onto the road as she ran.

I had recently written a report on the Pony Express for school and decided my best course of action would be to emulate the Pony Express riders and do a flying dismount. I took a deep breath, grasped the saddle horn, kicked my foot out of my right stirrup, and balancing myself, carefully slung my right leg over the saddle while grasping the cantle (the back of the saddle), and kicked my foot out of the left stirrup, hanging precariously off of Cindy's left side for a few moments (while she was still at a full gallop) before releasing my grasp on the saddle and dropping to the ground.

I landed hard on my feet, but one foot twisted, and I toppled over. But I had done it! I watched Cindy continue her headlong gallop until she neared the fence and came to a stop. *I should have known*, I thought to myself as I began to stand up. All was well until I put weight on the foot that had twisted, and pain shot up into my ankle. I let out a small scream of pain and crumpled back down to the ground.

Here I was, on a somewhat desolate road (it was cement but still in a fairly rural area), wondering what to do. I managed to scoot to the side of the road to avoid being run over and watched Cindy off in the distance, her head in the grass, munching contentedly. Fortunately, not much time passed before a car approached and rolled to a stop. A young man got out of the car and looked me over, evaluating the situation. He returned to his car and opened the rear passenger door, came back and scooped me up, and carefully laid me in the back seat. I handled all of this stoically, with nary a tear.

I don't remember much else, except that he brought me to his parents' house and some kind people helped me get settled in a recliner, with my leg elevated. Eventually, my daddy arrived, and as soon as I saw him enter the room, I burst into tears. Something about seeing my father made me feel safe, and I was able to express my emotions. He reassured me that Cindy had made it back to the barn and was being taken care of, and took me home. My next stop was the doctor's office.

So, long story short, I broke my ankle and had to be in a cast. Walking the halls of Terrace Elementary proved difficult, using crutches on the polished floors, but I managed. I remember being given a beautiful horse necklace about two inches wide to help me pass the time while I was bedridden. It was an arts and crafts kit with multi-colored jewels that I glued into the recessed pockets of the horse.

I was so excited when Mom and Dad took me and Eddie to see the cartoon version of Robin Hood (Robin was portrayed as a fox) while I was still on crutches. Afterwards, we went to our favorite local pizza place, Shakey's Pizza near Gibson's. I remember they had a piano and played old black and white shorts like Laurel and Hardy and the Three Stooges. We rarely went out to eat, so that was a very special treat. I didn't fully realize at that age how hard my parents worked to make me feel special.

Nancy riding with a cast, on Cindy; author photo

I convinced Mom and Dad to let me ride with my cast. Cindy was probably a little off balance by the added weight of it, but we managed okay.

More Horse Play

The front steps of Richardson Junior High; author photo

Back then, as I became more experienced, I became fearless on Cindy and would take my bay mare every-where, including riding up the steps to Richardson Junior High. As I sat on Cindy directly in front of the double doors, contemplating whether or not the hallways would be too slick for her hooves, the assistant principal caught me, making my decision an easy one.

Nancy with her horse Cindy and a barn buddy in the backyard of the house on Rorary; author photo

I lived and breathed riding my horse. I would ride her to our house on Rorary, and Mom would let me keep her in the backyard overnight. We would place our order from horseback in the drive-thru of Dairy Queen and pick up our orders at the drive-thru window. Cindy loved French fries!

I had my horse for about two years, but the time came when we could no longer afford her. I remember the last day I went to the barn. Both my mom and dad went with me. I got out of the car, grabbed her halter, and started walking through the pasture. There must have been five bay horses off in the distance but I knew exactly which one was Cindy and walked directly toward her.

Her head popped up from grazing, and she started walking toward me. In hindsight, that must have been very hard for my mom and dad to watch. Mom had a trophy made for me with a horse on it and a plaque that said, "Better to have loved and lost, than to never have loved at all." Looking back through a much more mature lens, it amazes me as to the lengths my mother and father went to give me the gift of a happy childhood and how hard my mom worked to comfort me when life got hard.

I was still very fortunate in that I was able to continue riding. My friend Katherine found a horse for me to ride over in Buckingham, the small town adjacent to Richardson, where many people had enough land to keep livestock. A big Appaloosa gelding named Hey Boy was made available to me. Back in those days, no one worried about liability and cheerfully shared what they had. That was the spirit of Richardson and Buckingham.

I have two very specific memories of riding Hey Boy. Katherine on her Appaloosa named Rustler, her friend on his buckskin Missouri Fox Trotter named Danny, and me on Hey Boy, were riding next to Plano Road near Richardson Square Mall. I don't know what got Hey Boy going, but he started bucking, right in the middle of Plano Road. Fortunately, traffic came to a halt, the rodeo didn't last too long, and I managed to stay on, even bareback.

Nancy Golden

*The railroad bridge over Bowser Rd that Nancy and her
friends rode their horses across; author photo*

Another time, we were riding along Belt Line Road near
the intersection of Belt Line and Bowser. Anyone growing up
in Richardson knows that there is a railroad track with metal
sides forming a bridge suspended over the busy traffic on Belt
Line (which is still there today). Katherine and her friend
reined their horses to climb up the steep, rock-laden side of the
tracks next to the bridge. Of course, I couldn't be chicken. I had
to follow.

Before I knew it, we were walking our horses single file over
that bridge, our legs hanging close to the metal walls on either
side, traffic rushing underneath. I can still close my eyes and
feel Hey Boy's furry sides and the rhythm of his walk, praying
the loud hollow noise of the horses' hooves clopping wouldn't
set him to bucking. I must admit it is one of my very favorite
memories—once I got to the other side—with fully earned brag-
ging rights.

Family Horse Play

Yee Haw! Mom riding Fury, the barn Shetland pony;
author photo

W e really did have the best of both worlds. While we lived in Richardson proper with all of its conveniences, Richardson was still semi-rural, with cotton fields and pastureland not far from our home, and everyone enjoyed a day at the barn once in a while.

Dad riding Cindy, with Nancy and Mom looking on;
author photo

Dad loved to ride and did so every chance he got.

Eddie riding Cindy; author photo

Eddie wasn't horse-crazy like me, but he still liked to ride and was fearless.

Eddie taking Mom for a ride; author photo

Mom was pretty fearless, too. She was always ready to try new things. Here she is riding Fury bareback.

Eddie and Nancy hanging out at the barn; author photo

Backyard Fun

Our backyard was ever-evolving as Mom adjusted it for our grade levels. Two metal posts spaced several yards apart served to hold a clothes line. Eddie and I became experts at running pell-mell through the backyard while avoiding those posts.

Eddie and Nancy playing on the two-seater with Zipper;
author photo

Our swing set provided hours of fun. I remember the day Mom and Dad bought it and put it together—we were so excited! We especially liked the two-seater at the far end. Sitting across from each other, we could push down with our feet on the pedals and get it going pretty fast.

Brandy and Herbie on the back porch; author photo

We were blessed with our furry companions that resided in the backyard. While being outside dogs, Mom and Dad made sure they were able to be shielded from the elements with a dog house, and on really bad weather days, they were allowed to come inside.

Zipper was our first dog, a short-haired Heinz 57 pup that was also an escape artist. Many a day, we would come home from school to find he had gone exploring and had to roam the neighborhood until we found him.

Growing Up with Eddie

Eddie and Nancy playing with Brandy; author photo

Brandy (a sweet little black/tan dog) and Herbie (a small collie mix) came next and were buddies. Eddie and I spent lots of time in the backyard together, playing with them.

Sprinkler fun on a hot summer day; author photo

We loved to play in the sprinkler on hot days and eventually got an above-ground swimming pool on the patio, which everyone enjoyed. It wasn't very large, but could hold our family, and was a precursor to our Terrace Swimming Pool days.

Nancy Golden

Screened In play area; author photo

Mom was very creative in making our backyard a haven. At one time, she had a screened in play area so that we could be outside but avoid the hot Texas sun's rays and mosquitoes. It was a large screened-in area like a tent, with a table and chairs inside.

Mom and Dad also bought a full-size tent, and we would have family campouts in the backyard. During the Fourth of July, if we weren't having a picnic at Heights Park, we would celebrate in our backyard with a barbecue, watermelon, and fireworks. One year, Mom and Dad invited the neighbors, and they were all sitting around the backyard in those folding chairs with the plastic strips. Us kids were running around with sparklers. When it got dark, the adults lit off fireworks. One of them (a flying spinner firecracker) seemed to target me, and I ran as fast as I could into the little room that served as a storage area, accessible from our backyard. Fortunately, the spinner didn't follow me in!

Growing Up with Eddie

Eddie and Nancy playing catch in the backyard; author photo

Eddie playing basketball in the backyard; author photo

Eddie and I spent many happy hours in our backyard, playing catch, tag, and basketball.

One year, I decided to plant a garden, and dug up a section of the yard. I dropped lettuce and radish seeds into the furrows I had created, and made sure to pull the weeds that popped up every few days. My gardening endeavor was fairly successful, and I was so proud when lettuce and radish leaves started to emerge from the ground.

Finally, it was time to harvest! The radishes had really

taken off, but I was very sad to discover—I don't like their taste (I'm not sure why I didn't know that before I planted them). I still had a lot of fun walking up and down our block, proudly handing out bunches of radishes to all of our neighbors.

Cereal Box Prizes and Space

Mom would let us pick out a box of cereal during our weekly shopping trips. Eddie would invariably choose Quake or Captain Crunch. While I may have been tempted by the toy to be found inside (advertised on the box), I had a fascination with the cereal that had a cute Martian on the front, and so usually chose Quisp, regardless of the prize. Even then, I had a love of space.

As soon as we brought all of the grocery bags inside and put them on the table, we would dig through them, grab our cereal boxes, and get a big bowl out of the cupboard in the kitchen and place it on the counter. We took turns, dumping the cereal out of the box and into the bowl until we located the prize, then poured the cereal back into the box. We may not have had much money growing up, but the small pleasures in life (like digging for the toys in cereal boxes with your brother) are some of life's best moments.

Astronauts of Apollo 11 jigsaw puzzle; author photo

My love of space manifested in other ways, too. I only have a fuzzy memory of watching the Apollo 11 Moon landing on our black and white TV since I was just six years old, but Tang was a morning staple inspired by the astronauts. As a family, we did a jigsaw puzzle of the Apollo 11 Moon landing, which lived in different rooms of our house over the years (and hangs in my living room today).

Eddie's Fish and Nancy's Rat

Eddie with his aquarium; author photo

E ddie's love for fish began very early, and he had his own aquarium that he took care of. His paper route money helped with the cost of his fish-keeping hobby, and Eddie was always messing with his tank, making sure that everything was operating properly and that the fish were doing well. He developed a fondness for angelfish that followed him into adulthood.

Penelope the rat; author photo

On the other hand, I chose a mammal to befriend, more specifically, a black-hooded rat I named Penelope. My friend Katherine also had a rat named Butterscotch (with a butterscotch colored hood), and the two often played together in the "Rat Ranch" Katherine and I made out of an old dresser and painted baby blue. Rats make great pets; they are friendly, inquisitive, will sit on your shoulder, and are nowhere as prone to bite as hamsters and gerbils. And speaking from experience, if they run under the couch, you can lure them out with a piece of skinny licorice.

Treats

E ddie and I had some favorite treats we would make when Mom and Dad were not around. The ingredients we needed were usually readily available from the weekly shopping.

Cinnamon Toast: Get out a flat pan from underneath the oven and heat the oven to 350 degrees. Butter six slices of bread and place the bread in the pan. Sprinkle liberal amounts of sugar on top of the butter, then sprinkle cinnamon on top of the sugar until the surface area of the bread is reddish brown. Place the pan in the oven and allow the bread to cook, checking frequently. When the cinnamon and sugar are melted into the bread and the bread has taken on a golden-brown color, turn off the oven and remove the pan. Best eaten while hot!

Pan-fried Donuts: Get a roll of biscuits out of the refrigerator, fully understanding there may be consequences later for doing so. Get a brown paper lunch bag and dump a bunch of sugar in it. Heat up a big pan of vegetable oil (whatever is in the cupboard). Open the roll of biscuits and take each biscuit and stretch it out so there is a hole in the middle. Try to make them look like donuts. When the oil is hot, drop the donuts in the oil. Watch them while the dough cooks and expands. They will have to get pretty dark in order for the dough to cook all the way through.

When they look like they are cooked, drop 1-2 at a time in the paper bag and shake. The sugar in the bag will adhere to the outside of the donuts. Have a plate ready to place them on. You'll have to wait a little bit for them to cool down enough to eat without burning your mouth.

'70s Comfort Food: grill cheese sandwich and tomato soup; author photo

Grill Cheese Sandwiches: Self-explanatory

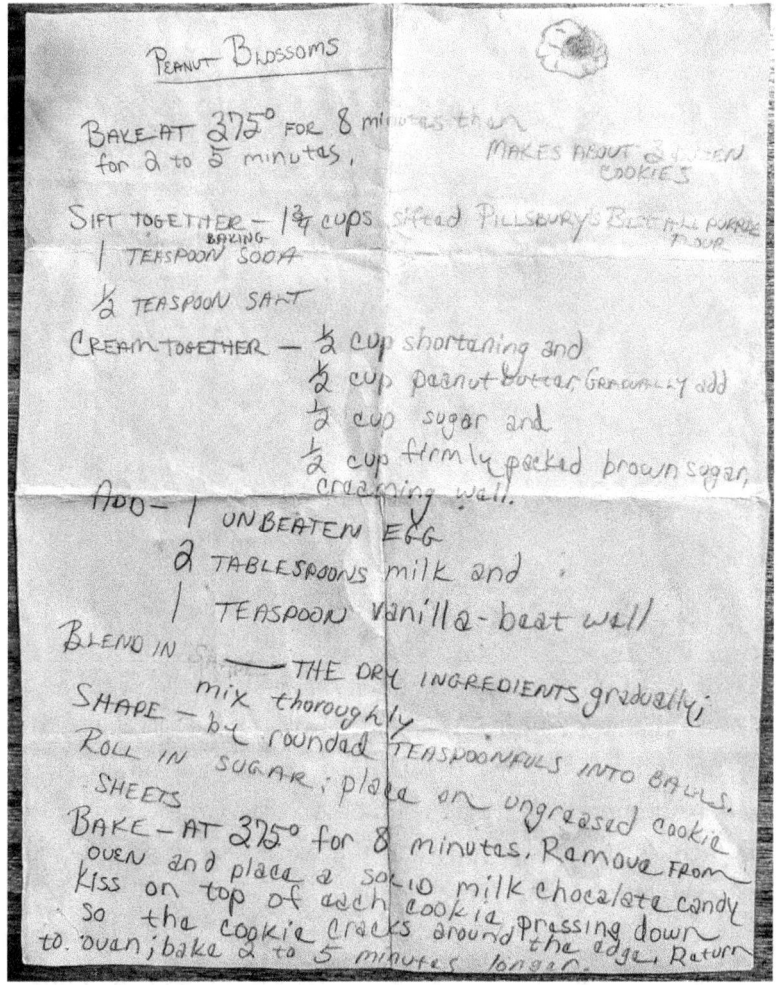

Peanut Blossoms recipe; author photo

Peanut Blossom Cookies: Pardon the messy look, but this is old! I started making these cookies in around the 6th grade (that's my handwriting) and loved to bake them around the holidays and for special occasions, or just because. I thought it was so much fun to press the Hershey Kisses into the cookie dough.

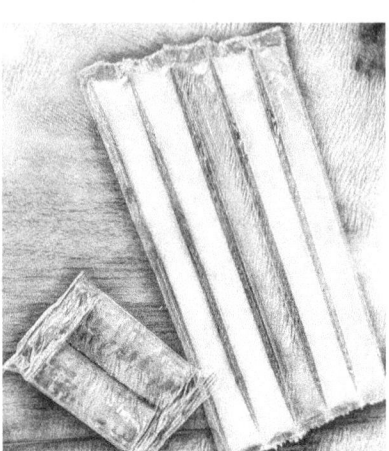

Store-bought treats; author photo

Flavored ice pops were a summer staple—Mom kept a box of them in the house for us. We would freeze some of them in the freezer and tear off our favorite flavor, for a cool summer treat on hot summer days. Eddie liked cherry-flavored best (red) and my favorite was grape (purple). We would eat all of those up before switching to the other colors.

Our other favorite store-bought treat was "Little Debbies" pastries and cakes. Mom would rotate the different kinds— Swiss Rolls and Nutty Bars were some of our favorites.

Terrace Shopping Center

*Terrace Shopping Center Grand Opening - Richardson
Echo 1958; courtesy Richardson Public Library*

One of the best things about living on Rorary Drive is that Eddie and I could walk to Terrace Shopping Center. Mom and Dad gave us a weekly allowance of 25 cents in elementary school. We would walk down Rorary Drive to where it dead-ended into La Salle Drive and an apartment complex.

Apartments on La Salle Drive; author photo

My sister Janet and her husband lived in those apartments
with their kids, and I would go visit them sometimes or drop by
for a snack. We would turn left on La Salle and right on
Terrace Drive, where we would soon be able to cut through the
parking lot to Skillern's and onto the shopping strip. I
remember Skillern's had a soda fountain, which was tempting,
but we usually made our way down the strip to M.E. Moses,
our local five-and-dime store. M. E. Moses had everything you
could ever want, from feminine products (When I was older, I
thought I would die with embarrassment when Mom made me
go into the store and buy my own—I just knew EVERYONE
had to be watching me!!) to model cars, paint supplies, and live
goldfish in a bowl! When Eddie got birthday money, he would
spend an hour going through the car and airplane models and
pick out his next project.

My brief career as a criminal started and ended at M.E.
Moses. The checkout stand was near the front doors and across

154

from the candy counter. Rows upon rows of candies (starting with the least expensive hard candies at the bottom, and more expensive Hershey bars toward the top) were stacked there. I was in the store with my dad, and I think I was probably in first grade. I looked around and then stuck one of the hard candies that was within my reach in my pocket. When my dad came to the counter to pay for his selections, the checker informed him that I had stolen a piece of candy. Busted! Dad turned to look at me, and I burst out crying. I reached into my pocket and gave the checker the piece of candy. That was the first and last time I have ever stolen anything, except for coins from Eddie's piggy bank when he wasn't home—but that's another story.

Summertime at Terrace Pool and Park

Richardson swim tag; courtesy Kelly Graf-Perkins

Richardson swim tag; courtesy Sandra Hamilton Husmann

Nancy Golden

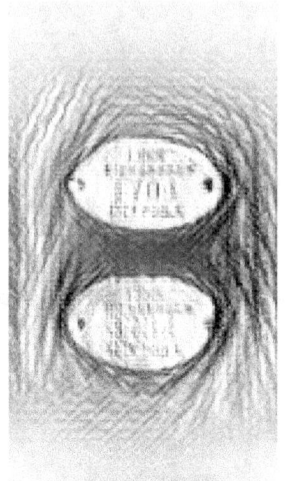

Richardson swim tag; courtesy Deborah Nemitz

Every summer we looked forward to spending our days swimming at Terrace Swimming Pool. Mom set aside money in May to buy the stamped piece of metal tag that came in a different shape and color each year—granting the owner access to Richardson swimming pools for the entire summer. I was always so proud of my sewn-on swim tag! I felt like a VIP shouting, "Tag!" as I bypassed the line at the entry counter.

Alley leading to Terrace Swimming Pool; author photo

Growing Up with Eddie

I grew up walking down the alley that ran alongside Terrace Elementary to Terrace Swimming Pool and swimming all day. I'd walk home to make a bologna and mustard sandwich for lunch, then walk back up to the pool to swim some more.

Terrace Swimming Pool; courtesy Richardson Public Library

"Marco!!" "Polo!!"

"Chicken on the high board!!"

I remember the high board—I wanted to learn how to do a forward flip off of it, but I didn't want to practice in front of my friends (and let them see my belly-busters), so I got a ride to Cottonwood to practice on their high board. I can remember feeling my heart race in apprehension as I climbed the high board ladder that seemed to go up forever and gingerly making my way to the end of the diving board. Looking down, I could see the rope with floats that marked the far edge of the diving area. I was determined, and spent the day flinging myself off the edge of that diving board. Once I got it down, I went to Terrace Swimming Pool and had a great time showing off my newfound ability to do a forward flip off the high board to my friends.

Occasionally, in the field in front of Terrace Swimming Pool during the summer, a marionette wagon would set up for free puppet shows in the park, and we would eagerly gather and sit cross-legged on the grass to watch. Arts and crafts classes were also offered in the park next to the tennis court. Eddie and I each had a wooden tennis racket, and once in a while we would head over to the courts and play.

When the swimming pool finally closed for the summer, we would climb over the tall chain link gate that locked up the pool entrance to get a closer look—it was always filled with frogs and tadpoles.

Heights Recreation Center

Learning ballet at the recreation center; courtesy vlrondon / pixabay.com

We loved going to the Heights Recreation Center on Arapaho Road. It was a magical place with so much to do! I took ballet lessons when I was in elementary school. I loved playing sports, and these classes were Mom's efforts to make me more ladylike. I remember struggling into my leotards, putting on my ballet shoes, and practicing my pliés. It was at the Rec Center that my mom patiently taught me how to play ping pong. She instilled in me a lifelong love of the game, and I have taken great joy in doing the same with my own son.

The Apple Doesn't Fall Far From the Tree

Our beautiful Mom; author photo

I miss my mom, every day. I was looking in the mirror this morning, and I could see her features in my own face—the way her face would crinkle with lines etched by life's trials complemented by the wrinkles engraved from a lifetime of smiles. How her eyes would squint a bit when she smiled—one more than the other, and with a twinkle in her eyes. I felt joy shoving my grief back into its corner. I am my mom's legacy!

Mom looked like a movie star; author photo

Funny thing about the aging process. I am finding this season of life has challenges my younger version could not begin to fathom, but also blessings that I am very grateful for. I remember Mom's jovial disclosure of her age on every birthday – "I'm 29!" I have chosen to keep my hard-earned grey wisdom highlights visible, whereas she had chosen to keep her red hair for several decades before letting go of her fiery crown. Either way, she was, and is, beautiful.

Mom had a hearty laugh and a great sense of humor. She lit up any room she was in, and she took much joy in music. I love the video we made of Mom singing while Phil and I danced in our kitchen after coming home from a Christmas Eve service.

Mom and Nancy - she had a way of making everything fun; author photo

When I look back on the impact she had on my life and her steadfast love, I feel so grateful that God gave her to me to be my mom. Cheerleader, teacher, confidante, nurturer, she was always there with a smile, a hug, and a word of wisdom. She was also there through every bump I experienced, even when they were the results of my own poor decisions.

Mom had a strong influence on my life. She would often say: "You have to have trust and faith," "Don't worry twice," "Take some honey," "Think happy thoughts," and always in times of trouble – "It's not a forever thing," and "Lord, grant me the serenity..." So when asked to speak at a ladies' ministry event at Living Word Global Church, Mom came to mind. She leaves a beautiful legacy in all of the lives she has touched, and I knew it was a great opportunity to share with others the wisdom my Mom had garnered throughout her life and had shared with me.

Our lifetime on Earth is short, and while we think we will have time to be with our loved ones, the truth is, the day the Lord calls them home will always be sooner than we think or want. Romans 14:8, "If we live, we live for the Lord; and if we die, we die for the Lord. So, whether we live or die, we belong to the Lord," gives me much comfort, because I know she is with the Lord—but I do miss her daily.

Don't neglect time with your loved ones, because tomorrow is not promised to any of us. The cherished memories of our many times together provide comfort until we are reunited again in Heaven.

Mom's wisdom has carried me through some difficult times, and I think her words will bless you, too. When you find yourself anxious about something that hasn't happened yet and may not, remember, "Don't worry twice."

When you are going through hard times, tell yourself an important truth that I know my mom would tell you: "It's not a forever thing." You will get out the other side to a place of blessing. It might take a while—but stay strong and hold onto your faith. You will get there.

And when you do that, I am quite certain my mom will be smiling down from her heavenly home.

Mom, I love and miss you, so much!!

Stealing and Confession

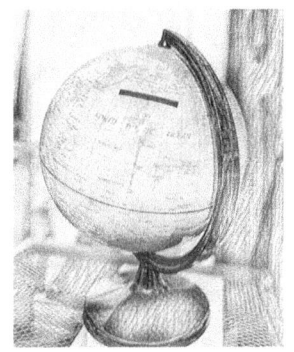

Eddie's piggy bank; author photo

Remember the incident I mentioned about stealing some candy in M.E. Moses? Well, apparently, my life of crime wasn't completely over, but I figured stealing from my brother didn't count. I would wait until no one was home (and make sure it was a day when Eddie was at football practice) and would slip into his room. A small metal globe of the world with a slot in the top served as his piggy bank. It resided in his bed-stand on the bottom shelf. I would sit cross-legged on the floor and pick it up. Turning it upside down, I grasped the edges of the plastic circular piece on the bottom and rotated it so that it would come off. I then proceeded to shake the globe until I managed to shake it enough for some coins to drop through the opening. I didn't want to be greedy, but I did want enough for a candy bar, so I usually limited myself to fifteen or twenty cents.

Which brings me to confession...specifically at St. Paul's Church. As a kid, I had a vague understanding of sin but had trouble defining my own. To make matters worse, all of the priests knew my dad, and so they knew it was little Nancy Venetucci on the other side of the screen, making me feel very self-conscious and awkward. Confessing to stealing from my brother's piggy bank solved that problem. I had a sin ready to go! I think I was covered by Matthew 18:3 back then, and fortunately, I have a more mature perspective today...

Venetucci Family Christmas Recipes

Mom and Dad: Two traditions bound by love; author photo

B eing half Jewish and half Italian was a huge advantage during the holidays. While we did not celebrate Hanukkah specifically (it usually falls somewhere around late November or December), Mom would put out our menorah, and we enjoyed food from both sides of our family. Dad cooked lasagna once a year, at Christmas. He would make several trays, and we always looked forward to it. I don't know the recipe, but I remember he would make the sauce from scratch and include little balls of Italian sausage.

I carry on that tradition in our family, although I use my own variation of a recipe I found on the back of a lasagna noodle box, and I don't make the sauce from scratch. My son Josh looks forward to it every year. When he is home, he helps me cook it, and we have a lasagna uncooked noodle sword fight as part of the fun. While not exactly authentic, it is definitely a family tradition carried forward with love:

Serving of lasagna; author photo

The Venetucci/Golden Lasagna Recipe

I always make two pans so we can have one pan for Christmas dinner and freeze the other one for another occasion.

2 lbs ground beef (I always buy extra lean ground beef or ground turkey for a healthier version)

1 large jar/jug of spaghetti sauce (in the neighborhood of 65-67 oz. depending on the brand). I don't make my own sauce, but every year I examine the variety of sauces at the grocery store and pick one that "speaks" to me. I usually select Prego traditional, but have tried a variety of different sauces over the years.

3 cups of water

30 ounces of ricotta cheese

24 ounces shredded mozzarella cheese

OPTIONAL: Additional 8 ounces of mozzarella cheese to top the lasagna during final bake

1 cup of grated Parmesan cheese

4 eggs

½ cup chopped parsley or, as an alternative, dried parsley flakes.

2 teaspoons salt

½ teaspoon of pepper

16 ounces uncooked lasagna noodles

Equipment: Frying pan, large cooking pot, 2 aluminum foil lasagna pans, aluminum foil

Preheat oven to 350 degrees.

Brown your ground beef or turkey in a frying pan and then drain thoroughly. Combine it with spaghetti sauce and water, and simmer it while you are doing the rest of the prep.

Next comes the filling. Combine the remaining ingredients except for the lasagna into a large bowl, stirring it until it has a creamy consistency.

Nancy Golden

Nancy and son Josh sword fighting with lasagna noodles;
author photo

Now is your opportunity to build your own family tradition. Pick out two of the uncooked lasagna noodles and hand one of them to a nearby family member or friend and challenge them to a duel. Proceed to dance around the kitchen in various sword-fighting poses. Laughter required, picture taking optional.

Have your two foil pans placed conveniently within range of the pot of sauce and the filling.

Have your lasagna sword-fighting partner commandeer one aluminum lasagna pan, and you take the other. Take turns doing the following:

Pour about 1 cup of sauce in the bottom of each pan, spreading it out to (mostly) cover the bottom of the pan.

Layer 3 uncooked lasagna noodles on top of the sauce.

Top noodles with about 1 ½ cups of sauce and then spread out about half of the cheese filling on top of the sauce layer (use a spoon or spatula to drop globs of filling onto the pan and spread it around so that the filling covers the entire pan). Estimating is fine; you don't have to measure the filling exactly.

*REMEMBER: *Since you are doubling the recipe, you will actually be using ¼ of the cheese filling you made for this layer in each pan**

Continue taking turns with another layer of noodles, sauce, and cheese filling.

Take turns topping with a final layer of noodles and remaining sauce.

Cover each pan with aluminum foil and place in the preheated oven. One pan would cook for 55-60 minutes, but since we have two pans, we will add 10 minutes to the cook time to adjust for the doubled mass to be cooked, so plan on a cook time of 65-70 minutes.

Remove foil (If you would like your lasagna to be extra cheesy, you can top each pan with an optional ½ cup of shredded mozzarella cheese). Bake another 10 minutes.

Remove from oven and if to be eaten immediately, allow to stand for 10 minutes to make it easier to cut.

NOTE: Lasagna refrigerated and served the next day is wonderful because all of the flavors seem to deliciously blend into each other. I often make lasagna the day before for that reason, and also because it is nice to not have to cook the same day all our relatives descend upon our home for Christmas dinner. A nice salad mix and garlic toast are perfect complements to this favorite holiday meal. The second pan gets frozen so that it is ready to go for the next special family occasion.

Bagels during Christmas Time

I already mentioned the bagels that we'd get every Christmas. Mom would buy cream cheese with chives and lox to accompany our bagels. I am salivating just thinking about it— that was truly a special treat! Sadly, our favorite Jewish deli and restaurant, Bagelstein's on Spring Valley Road in Richardson, no longer exists. However, there are several good options. Our current favorites are authentic kettle-boiled bagels from Just Bagels, located in Brooklyn. They ship right to our door. My sweet sister-in-law Jane frequently surprises me with a box; her thoughtfulness, and the delicious bagels, warm my Jewish heart.

You can get bagels at almost any grocery store, but I encourage you to seek out a Jewish deli in your neighborhood and try some from there—the authentic flavor just can't be beat. Lox (cured salmon) may not be to your taste, but make sure and add a generous dollop of cream cheese to a toasted bagel—your taste buds will thank you!

Egg Salad

You may not realize this, but egg salad is a traditional Jewish recipe. It is often enjoyed during holidays or for everyday meals, and we include it in our holiday traditions as well. There is both comfort and nostalgia to be found in this simple Jewish cuisine.

Ingredients:

10 eggs

Mayonnaise

Seasonings if desired (fresh dill, chives, salt, pepper, etc.)

Equipment:

Large pot, large mixing bowl

Boil the 10 eggs in a large pot for approximately 25 minutes. Dump the hot water and fill the pot with ice/cold water (this will make the eggs easy to peel).

Peel the eggs, then cut them up into small pieces. Stir in enough mayonnaise for your desired consistency. Add any seasonings and stir to distribute throughout the mixture. You can eat immediately or refrigerate—it's delicious cold! Make sure to store refrigerated in an airtight container.

Kasha; author photo

Kasha

A traditional Ashkenazi Jewish food, it may look strange since I can't think of any American counterparts. But oh my, we loved it when Mom decided to make a pot of kasha! It was one of Eddie's favorites, and today, I adore the sweet memories eating kasha evokes, as well as the unique taste.

Ingredients:

1 lb. of bow-tie noodles

½ cup of vegetable oil (and a bit more for drizzling)

3 large yellow onions, finely chopped

2 cups of chicken broth

1 cup kasha (roasted buckwheat)

Salt

Pepper

Fresh parsley (chopped)

Equipment:

Large pot to boil pasta, large pan to cook onions, medium pot to heat chicken broth and cook kasha, large bowl to combine all of the ingredients and serve (or rinse off the large pot used for pasta if for an informal gathering).

Add around a teaspoon of salt to a large pot of water and bring to a boil. Add the bowties and cook according to the directions, stirring occasionally until al dente (tender but firm and chewy).

Drain well and then transfer the bow ties to a large bowl. Coat the pasta by drizzling with vegetable oil and set aside.

Heat 1/2 a cup of vegetable oil and the onions together in a large pan over medium heat. Cover the pan and continue to cook, stirring occasionally, until the onions are soft (about 10 minutes). Uncover and season with salt. Continue cooking for around 10-15 minutes until the onions are caramelized (look golden).

Bring the chicken broth to a boil in a medium pot. Stir in the kasha, then simmer on low heat until the kasha is soft and the liquid is absorbed (14 to 20 minutes).

Remove from the heat and let stand covered for 5 minutes. Transfer the kasha to a bowl or the pot used for boiling pasta, along with the bow ties and the cooked onions. Season with salt and pepper and garnish with chopped parsley, if desired. Serve this delicious dish either warm or at room temperature.

The Christmas menu extended to other foods as well. No Venetucci special event occurred without spaghetti pie. This simple and unassuming dish was born when my ingenious mom found a way to stretch leftover spaghetti in such a way that left us all wanting more. As adults, whenever we had any sort of celebration, we would ask Mom to bring her famous spaghetti pie. Just the thought of it is wrapped up in sweet nostalgia for our childhood and our mother's love.

Spaghetti pie; author photo

Spaghetti Pie

Ingredients:

Pasta noodles (can be any type, but typically spaghetti). They can be leftovers from a pasta dinner, or you can buy a package. I usually use a 12-oz package of Skinner spaghetti if I don't have leftovers.

One egg

Salt

Pepper

Vegetable oil

Equipment: Frying pan, spatula

In a large bowl, mix your egg as if you are going to scramble it. Add your cooked pasta noodles and combine the egg with the noodles. If you have a lot of noodles, you may have to use two eggs. You will want it to be a drippy consistency so that the noodles are coated, but not too soupy. Add a few shakes of salt and pepper (you may want to adjust how much in future pies).

Heat up your vegetable oil in a pan that will hold the noodles while allowing about an inch of height for the sides to form. You can choose a larger pan for more noodles or do two smaller pies. You will want the end result to be an approximately inch-thick pie, so select your pans accordingly.

Blimpies; author photo

Blimpies *(Not sure who invented the name, but it's what we always called them)*

Ingredients:

Jumbo biscuits (no flaky biscuits, regular buttermilk)

Fresh kale

Either sliced mozzarella cheese from a block or shredded

Flour

Vegetable oil

Equipment: Rolling pin, cutting board, frying pan, tongs

Dust your rolling pin and cutting board with the flour. Take two biscuits and press them together as much as possible, and then roll them out as round as you can with the rolling pin. Once you have rolled it out, don't flip it. Take some fresh kale (not too much, just a few leaves) and also some mozzarella, and place them on the rolled-out biscuit. Make sure there is about an inch at each end with no filling. Now fold over the rolled-out biscuit (you will want to wet your fingertips so that you can do this more easily) and then seal it by squeezing the edges. Once you have all of your blimpies with their ingredients tucked inside and sealed all the way around, you will be dropping them into your frying pan to fry them. Put some vegetable oil in your frying pan so that it has about an inch of oil and heat it up so that it bubbles slightly. You will want to experiment with your heat setting (start on medium and progress to medium-high if they are taking too long to cook).

You can put as many blimpies in the pan as you can fit comfortably while giving them room to puff out. Keep checking the outer biscuit until it gets dark golden brown but not black. At that point, use your tongs to flip it over and continue to cook it until it is also dark golden brown but not burnt. As you are cooking it, you will see the blimpie begin to puff outwards. What you're trying for is a nice dark golden brown on both sides, with the biscuits being cooked all the way through and the inside cheese melted.

*Eddie was always an excellent cook and here he is
making blimpies; author photo*

You will have to experiment to get the blimpies the way you want them, and it can take a few tries, so just have fun doing it. After you have the blimpies cooked, you will want to place them on a plate that has paper towels on it, so that the oil can drain.

If it's like our house, they will fly off the plate and get eaten up fairly quickly, but in the rare case that there are leftovers, be sure to refrigerate them.

Pro Tip: If you find that you are unable to cook the biscuit thoroughly all the way through when you are deep frying them because they start to burn, you can also deep fry them to a golden brown and then put them in the oven to finish baking the biscuit dough—Thanks, Eddie!

White Fish

Ingredients:

Wild-caught frozen fillets (either cod or scrod)—make it easy on yourself and buy a bag of individually wrapped, skinless, already cut thin fillets: A possible source to purchase them is seafood from Sam's Warehouse.

Buttermilk

Salt

Pepper

Flour

Vegetable oil

Equipment: Bowls for buttermilk and flour, frying pan or Frydaddy, tongs

Season flour with salt and pepper. Dip the fish fillet in buttermilk so that it is coated, then roll the fillet in flour. Gently fry in a frying pan (enough oil to immerse the fillet) or in a Frydaddy. When the fish is cooked and has achieved a golden-brown crust, place them on a plate that has paper towels on it, so that the oil can drain. We usually eat them right after frying. You can also store them in the refrigerator and reheat them to enjoy later, but they will be the tastiest right after coming out of the pan.

Italian Shrimp

Ingredients:

Shrimp: Make it easy on yourself—buy your shrimp already peeled and de-veined. I get medium-sized shrimp and rinse them off, then pat them dry with a paper towel.

Buttermilk

Salt

Pepper

Flour

Vegetable oil

Equipment: Bowls for buttermilk and flour, frying pan or Frydaddy, tongs

This is easy—just prepare the shrimp the same way you did the white fish:

Season flour with salt and pepper. Dip the shrimp in buttermilk so that it is coated, then roll them in flour. Gently fry in a frying pan (enough oil to immerse shrimp) or in a Frydaddy. When the shrimp is cooked and has achieved a golden-brown crust, place them on a plate that has paper towels on it, so that the oil can drain.

I think seafood is always best when first cooked (especially when it is fried), but you can refrigerate and reheat it.

Linguini with Clam Sauce (simplified)

This was not the main event, but just a sweet reminder of our Italian heritage, amidst all of the food being cooked. I think that is why we didn't make the sauce from scratch, but there are some amazing recipes out there you may want to try.

Ingredients:

The hardest part of this very simple recipe is finding the clam sauce. We didn't make it from scratch, although that is a wonderful option. We would use Progresso-brand red clam sauce. Two small cans per one box of linguini.

Simply heat up the clam sauce in a pot to a simmer and follow the instructions for cooking the linguini. Combine, serve, and enjoy!

Owens Spring Creek Farm Adventure

*Belgian horses from Owens Spring Creek Country Farm
in a parade in Richardson; author photo*

Once when we were in elementary school, Eddie offered to go with me to Owens Spring Creek Farm, the home of the huge horses that were a common sight pulling a wagon when Richardson had a parade. He knew I was crazy about horses. A huge barn was made up of stalls with openings for the horses that allowed them to hang their heads over the doors and look outside. The horses faced the area for the public to be able to see them and even pet them —glorious! The property was sprawling and perfect for picnics, located at the intersection of Plano Road and Lookout. It was almost five miles from our house by bicycle. I was so excited!

We packed bologna sandwiches, potato chips, and water in a canteen. Eddie and I rode our bicycles, and I'll never forget that trip; my big brother leading the way as we navigated the streets of Richardson, stopping to drink out of our shared canteen, and finally arriving at the entrance to that little piece of heaven.

The horses were mostly Belgian draft horses, gentle giants that often took part in parades or pulled a wagon for hayrides at the farm. It was also a working farm where Owens made their sausage. Pigs, goats, ducks, and other farm animals made their home on the grounds, but I mostly had eyes just for the horses. They would lean their giant heads over the door to their stall and accept one of the carrots I had brought from home. Nodding their heads as they chewed it up, they would lean back over the door and blow gently through their nose, allowing me to stroke the soft fur of their muzzle. Eddie roamed the grounds while I spent the majority of my time at the stables.

Getting hungry, we sat on the grass and ate our bologna sandwiches, then explored the farm together, skipping rocks in the pond and running after the geese. Finally, reluctantly noting that the time was 3:00pm and per Mom's instructions, we got back on our bikes and headed home.

The Bean Bag Incident

The den became our play area when we got the bumper pool table. I'm not sure what year it was, but I am guessing I was in around sixth grade when Mom and Dad let us get a pet ribbon snake. We agreed to name him Bojangles after the song sung by Billy Joel, Mr. Bojangles, and he lived in an aquarium against one wall.

One of my sweet memories with Eddie was building the stand to hold the aquarium. Fortunately, measurements were not critical since it wasn't holding water (besides a small plastic pond for Bo to refresh himself in), and between the two of us, we managed to find enough pieces of wood, a hammer, and nails to piece it together. I'm not sure why we decided to paint it black, but I'm guessing it's because we had some left over paint from some other household project. Bojangles enjoyed being handled and liked to zip around the bumper pool table. He would even disappear down one of the pockets and emerge out another one.

Another staple in the den was a brown bean bag chair. I remember being so excited when Mom bought it for us. Back then, bean bag chairs were so cool! It became a familiar option, and I am sure I must have plopped into it hundreds of times. So, what happened in the front yard is somewhat of a mystery.

I don't remember why we dragged the bean bag chair into the yard, but it must have been for some sort of game we had thought up. Most likely, we were taking turns running and diving onto it. That is definitely something we would do. At any rate, the bean bag chair was in the grass in the front yard, facing the porch that led up to our front door. Somehow, the bean bag exploded, and the yard became thick with what seemed like thousands of white Styrofoam pellets, the "beans" that used to be in the bean bag chair.

Eddie vacuuming bean bag pellets in the front yard;
author photo

Mom came out to check on us, and by the look on her face, we knew we were in big trouble. Our vacuum was not an upright but rather, a pale blue and white canister model. I still have this picture in my head of Eddie holding the vacuum's long tube as he walked around our front yard, sucking up those white pellets, while I picked up the shreds of brown bean bag cover.

Digging through old family photos for "Growing Up with Eddie," I ran across an actual picture Mom must have taken. I guess she found it humorous, although she wasn't about to let us know that at the time!

Crawdad Fishin'

Mom had made another jug of milk from the red and white Carnation powdered milk box she kept in the pantry, and it had chilled all night in the refrigerator. At times, we did not have much money growing up, but Mom was a genius with the money we had. I poured some into my Quisp cereal and munched it contentedly, still in my pajamas, daydreaming of what I was going to do with my day.

Summertime! The best time of the year!

It promised to be another typical Texas hot summer day. Mom had already left for work, and Eddie had plans to go play with his best friend, who lived a few streets over on Apollo Road. I had been swimming all day the day before. The phone rang, and I dropped my spoon and got up to answer it. I picked up the yellow handset and twirled the cord.

"Hello."

"Hi Nancy, what are you doing?"

I immediately recognized the voice of one of my good friends.

"I'm just finishing breakfast."

"Let's go crawdad fishin'!"

"Okay, same place?"

"Yeah. Can you bring some bacon? I can bring string and a cooler."

I paused, twirling the cord faster and thinking about the possible consequences if Mom noticed the missing slices.

"Sure."

"Okay, see ya there."

Click

I returned to my chair at the table and hurriedly finished my bowl of cereal. I placed it in the sink and opened the refrigerator, hoping that we had some bacon in the bottom drawer where Mom kept it. Success! The package was already opened and still three-quarters full. I could hear my mom's voice in my head, "Shut the door, you're letting all the cold air out," and reflexively shut the door and went into my bedroom to change.

I emerged from my room in an old shirt, cutoff blue jean shorts, and sneakers. I got the bacon out and peeled off two slices. From my experience, three slices missing would be noticed, but I could probably get by with two. I pulled out one of the lunch-sized paper bags Mom kept in the cupboard and dropped them in there. I stuck my pocketknife into my pocket, grabbed my house key from where I kept it in my dresser, and I was ready! I went outside and tossed the bag holding the bacon into the basket of my bike and headed toward Dorothy, where I could ride down the alley all the way to Lois Lane in front of Terrace Swimming Pool, turn left on Lois, and right on Apollo, which after a couple of blocks dead-ended at the railroad tracks at Bowser.

*Crawdad fishing by the railroad tracks at Bowser Rd,
where Apollo Rd dead-ended; author photo*

It was immediately obvious that a bunch of kids had the same idea—several bikes were lying scattered in the field near the tracks, their owners already down by the creek, wading in it or crouched along the sides, looking for crawdads. I grabbed my bag of bacon and dropped my bike alongside the others. I could hear voices and the occasional shout, "I got one!" rising in the air.

I made my way down to the creek and kicked off my tennis shoes so they wouldn't get wet. Six or seven other kids were wading in the water, dragging strings or sticks with bait through it, ready to pounce if a crawdad came their way. My friend showed up minutes later, a beat-up Styrofoam cooler in hand.

She slid down the side of the bank and turned the cooler sideways into the creek, filling it about a third of the way with water. I took out one of my slices of bacon and handed her a piece. She pulled out a ball of string from her pocket, and I cut off two pieces with my pocketknife. We tied our bacon pieces to our lengths of string and joined the other kids in the creek.

It was a beautiful sunny day, but the water was still cold, and the mud squished between our toes as we sloshed through it, heads bent in hopeful anticipation. From past experience, I headed to where some rocks were loosely resting next to each other, forming a little cave where a crawdad could hide. I dropped my bacon in a crack between the rocks, and pretty soon I was rewarded with a splash in the water as a crawdad snagged the bacon.

Crawdad Sighting!; courtesy gingerbreadmedia.online

Yes! Now, the fun part: Grabbing the crawdad without getting pinched. I squatted next to the rocks while holding onto the string with my left hand. I reached behind the two big pinchers with my right hand like Eddie had taught me, quickly grasping the crawdad right behind where they connected to its body, and lifted it out of the water with a grin.

The crawdad was squirming, swinging its claws, but I was out of reach. To my delight, it let go of the string, and the piece of bacon was still intact, saving me from having to use more of my bait. I swung my catch in the air to show him off while my friend cheered and then tossed him unceremoniously into the cooler. My first catch of the day made me eager to try again, and the morning passed quickly as we continued to fish for these lobster look-alikes.

About six crawdads later, we ran out of bait and decided to call it quits. My stomach was rumbling, and I was ready to go home and fix a bologna sandwich for lunch. Dirty, happy, and satisfied with my efforts, I waved bye to those that remained, climbed back up the bank, and got on my bike for the ride home. My friend always kept the crawdads. I don't know what she did with them, and I didn't really care—all I knew was that it sure was fun catching them.

I haven't strayed far from Richardson, now living in Carrollton. I'll never forget the time I enrolled my then 12-year-old son in Nature Camp, held on the same property that housed the Future Farmers of America—so despite being in a suburb of Dallas, this area was still fairly rural. On Parents' Day, my husband and I drove up to the camp. Much to my delight, they had a creek with crawdads, something not found in the more pristine green belts where we lived in Carrollton. I was so excited as I called my son over. One of my proudest moments as a mom was showing my son how to pick up a crawdad without getting pinched!

Bamboo Pole Inspiration

We had some bamboo poles that we used when we went fishing, and Eddie pulled them out one day and handed me one with a grin. "Let's play charge!"

I looked at him sideways, cocking an eyebrow. "Are you sure that's a good idea?" I hefted the bamboo pole, then turned it so I could see the circular end and studied it. "This could poke out an eye."

"Nah," Eddie shook his head. "We'll be careful."

We went out to the front sidewalk, our makeshift lances in hand. I jogged about three houses down toward La Salle Drive, and Eddie jogged three houses down toward Dorothy Drive.

We turned and gazed at each other, holding our bamboo poles by our sides. Eddie lifted his and yelled, "Charge!!"

I brought mine up and aimed toward him, and we both started running as fast as we could toward each other.

I don't know what I thought would happen after that, but what did happen was that Eddie's pole hit me first, right under my left eye. I dropped my pole and started wailing—it hurt!

Eddie dropped his pole and grabbed me to have a closer look. The expression on his face made me wail even louder—the end of his bamboo pole had left an imprint that was already bruising.

"Come on," Eddie pulled me urgently toward our house. "We need to show Mom."

Fortunately, Mom was home and immediately knew what to do. After a quick examination that assured her my eye was undamaged, she had me sit in my chair and put ice on the offending spot. I had stopped crying by that time, although Eddie continued to hover.

I must not have been hurt that badly because Mom included me in her stern lecture about participating in such foolishness, "Why, Eddie could have poked your eye out!"

Eddie was appropriately contrite, and by the end of the day, the swelling had gone down, although still leaving a tell-tale circle where Eddie's pole had landed. And of course, the next day was school pictures.

Key of Power, Book Three in the Dynamic Trilogy, by Nancy Golden; author photo

It's really true, writers often draw from personal experience when writing. This is a scene from the third book in my fantasy trilogy, Key of Power, and it was inspired by the "bamboo pole incident." It is especially poignant since I knew Eddie would not be with us much longer when I wrote it:

> "Your mother was amazing," the Swordsman leaned back, a smile tugging at his mouth as a childhood memory came to mind. "She was fiercely independent as a child." He shook his head and laughed. "You should have seen her when father told us we had to work the field. She was to throw seeds behind me as I plowed. She was very anxious to meet her friends and was doing her best to hurry me along when our horse decided he was done and would not move, no matter how much I shook the reins."

He gazed at Finn, his eyes sparkling as he replayed the scene in his mind. "She dropped her bag of seed, ran by me, grabbed the plow harness, and climbed aboard that huge horse's back. His name was Dobber. She started yelling and kicking with her skinny legs. It was like watching a flutebird trying to get a dragon moving. The funny thing was, that horse was so flabbergasted at her audacity that he leapt forward and pulled the plow with him.

"My hands were caught in the loops that I had made to hold the reins to the handles, and before I knew it, the plow turned over sideways as it continued to move forward, and I was going along with it." The Swordsman paused and lifted his left thumb to show Finn a faded scar running between the surface of his thumb and forefinger. "My hand got smashed between a rock and the plow handle. The scar has faded but never disappeared."

Finn, her eyes wide as she leaned forward listening with rapt attention, let out a breath. "Then what happened?" she asked.

The Swordsman gazed at the astonishingly familiar face in front of him. "The plow broke and left me in the dirt, but your mother managed to stay on Dobber. I never saw that big draft horse move so fast. She finally got him turned, and I clambered up behind her so we could ride home and get my hand doctored." He laughed. "I thought that after that, she wouldn't ride Dobber again, but to my surprise, it was quite the opposite. She and that big goofy horse became insepara-ble, and he would do anything for her. It was quite a sight seeing a pint-sized girl riding that big draft horse around the village with no saddle or bridle."

Finn closed her eyes and smiled as she pictured her mother as a young girl riding that huge horse. "Mother told me about Dobber, but she never told me that story." She opened her eyes and grinned at the Swordsman. "But she did tell me about the time you two found a couple of bamboo poles and decided to play charge." She pointed just below her right eye. "If you looked really closely, you could still see the circle of the end of the bamboo pole where you accidentally poked her with yours."

The Swordsman laughed at the memory. "Yes, it was not intentional, but Father took me behind the woodshed for it." He placed his hand over his heart. "Fortunately, your mother never held it against me."

"No, she didn't," Finn leaned forward and placed her small hand on the Swordsman's huge one. "She was always very proud of you and missed you terribly."

He smiled at his niece. "We have shared sorrow, Finn, but also joy. I am glad you have found me."

Finn sniffled and rubbed her eyes. "I am, too, Uncle Zander."

He gazed at her and shook his head in wonder. "You are so much like your mother." The Swordsman leaned forward in his chair, still smiling. "Come, we best go meet the others in the dining hall. It must be close to lunch time." His expression changed and his eyebrows knit together in concern. "We must understand what we are up against. Perhaps you can help us."

"That is why I came," Finn replied firmly, her eyes flashing with determination.

The Swordsman jerked back and looked carefully at his niece. "Yes, she is just like her mother," he mumbled to himself.

The big man shook himself and stood up. He reached out and awkwardly patted her shoulder. "Come then. Let's go join the others."

Nancy Golden

Nancy's school picture with the bamboo pole circle imprinted under her left eye; author photo

And if you look carefully under my eye on the right side of my school picture photo, you'll be able to see an imprint of the circle from the end of the bamboo pole where Eddie accidentally poked me with it...

Scouts

Cub Scout Eddie and Brownie Scout Nancy; author photo

E ddie and I both became scouts when we were in elementary school. Eddie started as a Cub Scout, moved on to being a Webelos, and ultimately, a Boy Scout. He loved scouting, and I can recall many fun events that he was involved in. Eddie and Dad built a car together for the Pinewood Derby when he was a Cub Scout.

Eddie, proud to be in his Cub Scout uniform; author photo

The races took place in the Terrace Elementary school cafeteria and were always exciting. Homemade pinewood cars were painted in a variety of colors and designs, and everyone gathered around the track and cheered during the races.

Sir Eddie the knight; author photo

It seemed there was always an adventure in store when Eddie went to Cub Scout meetings. His den mother was very creative, and his pack was always up to something fun.

We always attended the meetings when Eddie would be receiving an award. When he was a Webelos Scout, we went to the ceremony where he was awarded the Arrow of Light. I remember being in awe at the way the presentations were conducted, so solemn yet dramatic. The lights would go down in the auditorium and a drum was beaten for effect.

Eddie getting ready to go on a scouting adventure;
author photo

When Eddie transitioned into being a Boy Scout, he went on several camping trips and summer camp.

Letter to Eddie (from Nancy) at a Boy Scout camp at Lake Texoma; author photo

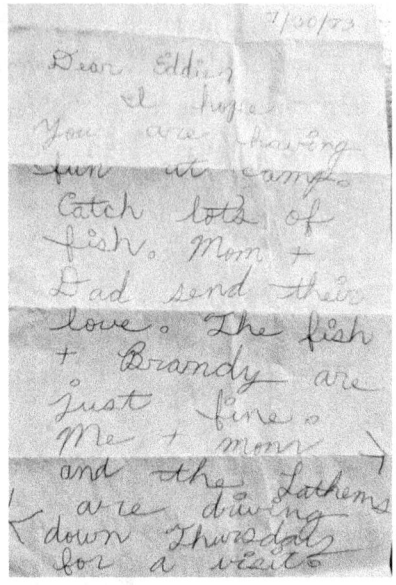

Actual letter, page 1; author photo

Actual letter, page 2; author photo

I always missed him and would write him letters.

*A craft Nancy made at one of her weekly Brownie Scout
meetings; author photo*

I was a Brownie Scout in elementary school. We had
weekly meetings and monthly activities that included going to
the Ice Capades, having a Christmas party, selling Girl Scout
cookies, visiting a hospital, roller skating, and a Father-
Daughter Banquet (each listed on the back of the plate above).

*Nancy in her Girl Scout uniform with Mom and Dad;
author photo*

Nancy Golden

Girl Scouts event at Huffhines Park; author photo

As a Girl Scout, I worked hard to earn my badges. We did a lot of activities including a field day with other scout troops representing different countries. Our troop represented Japan, and we made kimonos to wear to the event.

Performing the Scottish dance we worked hard to learn;
author photo

Another time, we learned Scottish dance steps and dressed up in kilts.

We also went on camping trips. Mom went on one with us, and she rapidly became a troop favorite. I have a precious memory of sitting around a campfire at night while she led everyone in singing "There's a Hole in the Bottom of the Sea."

Junior Honor Society and Shop Class

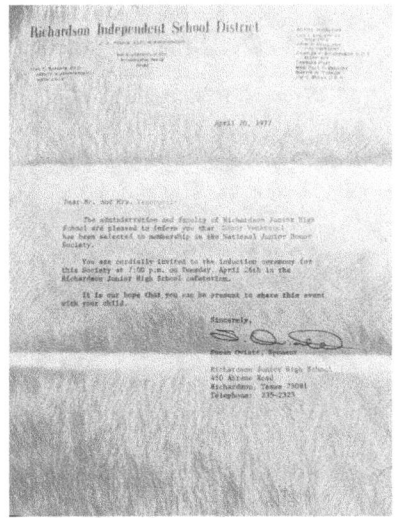

*Letter informing Nancy she was selected for the National
Junior Honor Society; author photo*

I n eighth grade, I received a letter from school in the mail, informing my parents that I would be inducted into the National Junior Honor Society.

NJHS program (front); author photo

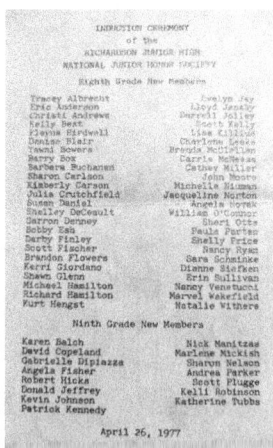

NJHS program; author photo

Mom was absolutely bursting with pride. As usual, Mom,

Dad, and Eddie attended the ceremony to see me honored, along with my classmates.

~

Bookshelf Nancy made in shop class; author photo

I always loved building things, and I was the only girl in my shop class at Richardson Junior High. I had so much fun using the woodworking tools that were made available to us. I built my dad a bookshelf (and stained it) that he kept in his office—he was very proud of it. That same bookshelf is now in my own office as a sweet reminder of my dad that I can see every day.

Summer Camp

Nancy sitting on her horse, Slick, at Camp Whispering Cedars; author photo

Eddie and I got to go to camp with the scouts every summer in elementary school, and as a teen in our youth group, I went to church camp with the Richardson East Church of Christ at Camp Goddard in Oklahoma.

I loved going to Girl Scout camp because it was before we

got my horse, and I was one horse-crazy little girl. I remember bringing home the brochures for Girl Scout camp. We had two choices: one focused on lake activities and the other focused on horses. No one needed to ask me which one I wanted to go to: Camp Whispering Cedars—here I come!

During camp, I would always wander back to the barn to be with the horses during other activities. The horse wranglers didn't shoo me away—I think I reminded them of their younger selves. We spent two glorious weeks riding horses and preparing for the play day that occurred at the end of camp. I got to learn how to pole bend for that event, and our parents drove up to watch.

Nancy with Appaloosa colt; author photo

One year, I was riding an Appaloosa mare who still had a foal by her side, and the next a flashy dun gelding named Slick. It took me a while to make friends with the other girls the first year (I didn't know the ones assigned to my cabin), but my mom's letters comforted me, and eventually I did, somehow earning the name "Bananas" although I can't remember why.

By the way, I happen to be the Frisbee Champion of Camp Goddard— two years in a row!

Letter from Nancy's mom; author photo

One of the wonderful things about our family is our devotion to one another. Letters flowed back and forth between me, Mom and Dad, and Eddie, just as they did when Eddie was at camp.

Vacation Bible School and Church

Faith was a fundamental part of being in community, growing up in Richardson. Every summer, it seemed every church offered Vacation Bible School, a fun time of games and crafts while learning about Jesus. If you couldn't get to the church, they would come get you in a van. It was a wonderful way to spend a summer day. It didn't matter if you belonged to a church or not, everyone was welcome. During my childhood, I attended St. Paul the Apostle Catholic Church, Richardson East Church of Christ, and First Baptist. Each contributed to my spiritual well-being.

*Getting ready for First Communion at St. Paul the
Apostle Catholic Church; author photo*

I have sweet memories of going to Mass with Dad and
Eddie (Mom attended St. Paul's for special events but usually
stayed home and had lunch ready when we returned). I also
went to CCD, and I can picture the Sister who taught us,
although I can't remember her name. She had a stern exterior,
but was really mushy inside. Dad always served as an usher,
along with a friend of his. I became friends with his friend's
daughter, and we often rode horses together. Eddie became an
altar boy—a big commitment with mandatory meetings during
the week. It was very special to receive the communion host
with him holding the communion plate.

Dad did not have a good singing voice, but that didn't stop
him from singing loudly. His favorite hymn was Amazing
Grace, I think because he was so grateful for God's grace in his
own life.

I love the comforting liturgy of Mass. We were handed
bulletins and white laminated cardboard mini-posters with the

words of the songs we would be singing. I loved (and miss now that it's been changed) the traditional, "Peace be with you." "And also with you." The cadence of kneeling, rising, repeating, and singing as the service flowed, and the entire congregation holding hands as we recited The Lord's Prayer together was a sacred act of worship.

I also remember during football season, we would often adjourn to the church cafeteria after Mass, to watch the Dallas Cowboys play.

As a teenager, my friend Katherine invited me to attend Richardson East Church of Christ. I became a member of the youth group, and our entire family started attending that church together. The youth group was amazing, serving to grow my faith and awakening in me a desire to study the Bible. It was a place of love and acceptance combined with fun activities while nurturing us spiritually—so important in the teenage years!

I made many lifelong friends in that youth group. Church camp took place at Camp Goddard and helped me to truly understand the atoning work that Jesus did on the cross for us. Attending Richardson East during my teenage years was a wonderful time of unconditional friendships, all of us devoted to Christ and to each other. I am also very grateful for the many Christian mentors who invested in us and our spiritual growth.

First Love

T eenage years are so hard. I was not a freak, a jock, or a
social (if you grew up during the '70s, these terms
need no explanation). I didn't fit in anywhere. By this
time, Eddie was hanging out with his own friends, and we
didn't see much of each other outside of our house. He was also
busy working at Dunkin' Donuts (we all looked forward to the
donuts he brought home after work) and then at Dairy Queen.

In the youth group at Richardson East, we did lots of
church activities, and I met a very nice, handsome young man.
Time went by, and he shyly asked me if I would like to go to a
movie. "Close Encounters of the Third Kind" had just come
out in theaters. I was so excited—my first date!

Mom helped me pick out my outfit. The weather was cold
and I had on a white, imitation fur coat. I felt like a princess
wearing it. His parents drove my date to our home, and he came
in and met my dad. They immediately liked each other.

I don't remember which parent drove us and which took us
back home, but I do remember sitting in Northwood Hills 4
theatre holding hands with my new beau. We probably shared

a popcorn and got Cokes, but the details are blurry. After that, we continued to date.

He would call me in the evening, and I would manage to stretch the telephone cord far enough to be able to talk in my own room. I was taking drama at RJHS and had decided I wanted to be an actress (that didn't last long!), and we used to each choose a part from a play and read it out loud, pretending we were acting. He also gave me my first Valentine's Day heart-shaped box of candy from a boy, along with a big, beautiful card.

Sadly, when I came back from my camping trip in the mountains because my dad had died, I broke up with my wonderful boyfriend. I remained closed off while I struggled with my grief. If I could see my first boyfriend today, I would thank him. Life changed after my dad was gone, and my life had many challenges, but I will always remember that sweet time of first love. It was a time of innocence, when I was treated respectfully and loved for who I was.

Mac n Cheese

A Blog Post I wrote in 2022:
A Mac N Cheesy Tradition

Serving of macaroni and cheese; author photo

Traditions are so important. They ground us, they bring comfort during turbulent times, they give us a sense of who we are, and that we belong. I would like to share something special that happened during our son Josh and his beautiful wife Naomi's visit this past week. I wanted to do something special with Naomi that honored our family's traditions and also pass one down to her. I reached out to my sister Janet to make sure I got the recipe right (Yes, Sis – I used Panko!) and bought the ingredients for making the macaroni and cheese that my mom used to make. She didn't make it very often, and so we were all very excited when she did. I remember the unique bread crumb crust on the top that everybody loved.

So this week, Naomi and I made Mom's macaroni and cheese together. It was a very special time as we chatted and together decided how much of what to put in it, since we didn't use any measuring cups. Naomi's grandmother had also shared a macaroni and cheese recipe for her to treasure. Naomi now has a recipe from my mom that she may not follow exactly, but is something for her to build off of (along with her grandma's recipe) that will carry a part of both of our families into the new family that she and Josh are creating together—and that is really cool!

I thank God for the gift of my daughter-in-love Naomi, and I'm so blessed by the times that we get to spend together.

If you don't have a family tradition to pass down, that's okay because you can start creating your own right now. And it doesn't even have to be family that you pass it to. The important thing about tradition is the love behind it, and that each of us can create our own as an expression of that love and give it to anyone. It's also good to remember that blessings are meant to flow in both directions. I can't tell you how much I look forward to the German pancakes Naomi makes for us whenever we get together for an extended visit—Yum!!

For those of you who are interested, I am including the macaroni and cheese recipe. If you choose to use it—feel free to tweak it and make it your own. And I know my mom will be smiling from Heaven because a tradition that she began in our family is being continued by others.

Leah Venetucci's Mac N Cheese

16 oz. large elbow macaroni

Approximately 1 cup of milk

Kraft Deluxe American Cheese (12 Slices)

Butter

Olive oil

Breadcrumbs (You can use plain or Panko)

9 X 12 glass baking pan

Lots of love

Cook the elbow macaroni as you normally would — boiling — straining — and adding a dollop of olive oil to prevent the macaroni from sticking together. Now would be a good time to start preheating your oven to 350 degrees.

Layered cheese slices; author photo

Place pats of butter on the bottom of the baking pan. You can also mix some butter in with the macaroni, although we settled for just the olive oil we had already added earlier. Layer half of the macaroni into the pan. Pour approximately half a cup of milk over the macaroni. Layer cheese slices on top of the macaroni. (For a richer recipe, you can add additional pats of butter on the cheese—being a bit health conscious, we chose not to do that this time and really didn't miss it).

Repeat with another layer of macaroni and add some more milk (this is now individual preference as to how you like the final texture to turn out—more milky or less milky...) and layer cheese slices on top of the macaroni.

Now the fun part—shake the container of breadcrumbs so that they cover the top layer of cheese. You can experiment with how thick a layer you like, but it doesn't take much to achieve the desired effect of a crispy, tasty top.

Bake for about 30 minutes (on the top rack is fine) until golden brown. Timing is not critical, but if you see the macaroni is getting crisp and you don't want to overcook it—you can also broil it for a few minutes (less than 5) to achieve the color of the crust you see in the pictures. If you choose to do this, the top will cook very quickly, so you will want to monitor it closely.

Macaroni and cheese; author photo

It is now ready to enjoy and, of course, refrigerate leftovers promptly. We also have a family tradition of praying over our meals, and we often end our prayer in a beautiful way – "Please bless this food and the hands that prepared it." I think we'll start including, "and thank you for the tradition of love behind it." Seems like a good idea, don't you think?

Richardson Public Library

*1978 Richardson Public Library in the winter; courtesy
Richardson Public Library*

Mom would take us to the Richardson Public Library, initially a red brick building on Tyler Street located behind the police station, consisting of two rooms separated by a circulation desk. She had already instilled in me a love for books, and the cramped aisles of books were a place of absolute delight. The library eventually moved to a new location (with a much bigger space) in 1970, on Arapaho Road.

We were even more amazed; the new location had an elevator!! We would ride the elevator for fun, and I remember getting out on the second floor to see all of the paintings—and was very surprised that we could even check one out! Being horse crazy, I checked out a painting with horses, and it hung in my room for two weeks before I had to bring it back.

Richardson was a place for horses in the '70s, including the library; courtesy Christopher Foster

Horses could be seen in the field behind the library, and it was also used as a staging area for those riding their horses in the city parades.

Our dad's Richardson Public Library card; author photo

I had an orange library card with a rectangular piece of metal. That was my ticket to other worlds! I would spend hours in that library and bring home stacks of books taller than I was.

Explorer Post 455

Richardson Junior High had so many great opportunities for kids. Extracurricular activities abounded. Eddie stayed focused on band, while I soon realized I was very limited talent-wise in that area. I was very active in sports at school (volleyball, basketball, and soccer), but I wanted to do something more. When I heard about co-ed scouting in the form of an Explorer Post, I decided to give it a try and immediately loved it. Explorer Post 455 was designated a "Woods and Water" post, which meant we would spend a great deal of our time outdoors. We had wonderful sponsors and teacher participants supporting us.

The trips we took canoeing down the Guadalupe River (white water) and the Brazos River (we practically walked it, but we had fun fishing) grew my outdoor competence, my self-confidence in what I was capable of, and my social skills; we all had to work together to be successful. These trips also nurtured my love of nature even more.

Being a member (and later an officer of Post 455) was especially meaningful during my time at RJHS, because during our much-anticipated mountain climbing trip to New Mexico and the Boy Scout Philmont Mountain Range in March of 1978, my father died unexpectedly while we were snowshoeing on Mount Baldy.

The news was relayed to our lead sponsor by radio, and he had the unenviable task of telling me. He asked me to hang back so I could help him put on his snow shoes as an excuse. He was sitting on a log in the snow, and as I worked on the buckles, he leaned over and put his arm around me, drew me close, and told me the news. We sat on that log until my tears quit flowing and then headed out to meet the others who had snowshoed to a place a few miles up the mountain to where a jeep could reach us. As we broke through the trees, I could tell by the expressions on everyone's faces that they already knew. One of the other girls volunteered to go back with me.

Obviously, my world turned upside down that day, as it did for my family. I have chosen to end my memories here, because this book is all about the carefree, idyllic period of my child-hood during the '70s. The death of a beloved parent changes everything, but I will never forget the love and compassion shown to me through the sponsors, teacher volunteers, and fellow Explorers during that very difficult time.

Best Daddy in the World

Eddie and Nancy on a Sunday afternoon with Daddy;
author photo

s a young adult, I didn't talk about my dad much, except to say he died when I was almost fifteen. The years after his death were traumatic as my mom, brother, and I struggled to maintain a semblance of family identity. My brother and I were rebellious teenagers, and having our anchor dislodged unexpectedly made for very rough sailing for all of us. As the years went by and I dealt with the consequences of my immature decisions, I thought of my dad less and less.

I'm grateful that my mom remained steadfast—she was always there for me, no matter what. But for some reason, we didn't talk much about Dad. We may have done the occasional reminiscing about a past holiday or event, but we didn't dwell on his absence. Perhaps each one of us had a hole in our heart we didn't know how to fill, so it was easier to ignore it rather than to acknowledge it. Back then, there wasn't anything like grief counseling available. We were left to deal with it the best we knew how, which often wasn't very good.

I was in elementary school when my dad took me on a Daddy-Daughter date. I remember putting on my best dress, and I was amazed that it was just us at a fancy restaurant. I felt so special!

He used to insist we be on time for our bedtime, and if we were one minute late, he would get mad at us. I would be so upset that I made him angry, I would lie in my bed and cry, then creep down the hallway where I could see him through the cracked hallway door, sitting in his recliner watching television. He would see me peeking at him and would tell me to come over, so he could give me a hug.

He bought his horse-crazy little girl her own horse, even though we didn't have much money growing up. One time when I fell off my horse and broke my ankle (I was around eleven years old), a young man found me and put me in his car and brought me to his mother's house. I had not shed a single tear until I saw my daddy in the doorway—then I burst out crying because my emotion at seeing him was so overwhelming.

Nancy and Daddy; author photo

I was truly Daddy's little girl. I loved to draw pictures for him that always had the caption "Best Daddy in the World."

I remember a science project my dad helped me with. He sold safety products including yard lights, and he helped me build a street with houses and yards made of cardboard in a large box. We wired a miniature yard light in front of each of the houses, so that they lit up when I flipped a switch.

Mom, Eddie, and I would wait for Dad to come home from work so we could all eat dinner together. Later in the evening, we would often sit in the living room. We each had our own spot and I would curl up in mine and read while we watched nighttime television that included The Tonight Show with

Johnny Carson, Saturday Night Wrestling, and The Wonderful World of Disney.

Dad with Nancy and Eddie, and the Easter bunny cake
Nancy made for Dad; author photo

I made my dad a bunny rabbit cake for Easter one year and was very excited to give it to him.

Some of Dad's favorite sayings growing up:

"Two wrongs don't make a right."

"If you don't know, it's simply awful. If you do know, it's awfully simple."

"Life is hard, yard by yard. Inch by inch, it's a cinch."

Family was very important to Dad, and he rarely let me or Eddie spend the night with our friends. He always said we needed to be home with family.

One of my fondest memories is knowing that no matter the event, whether it was one of my soccer games or band concerts (I played clarinet, but I wasn't very good), Mom, Dad, and Eddie would be in the audience to cheer me on. And we would all be there for Eddie.

I remember so many summer nights at Terrace Park,

watching Eddie play baseball—he was the catcher. I was always impressed when he would grab his mask and yank it off his head, so that he could see the pop fly and catch it.

The Children's Living Bible; author photo

Dad bought me my first Bible—I read it all the way through. I loved the illustrations that were sprinkled throughout its pages.

He made every Christmas special with his famous lasagna and would take us to Midnight Mass on Christmas Eve. He didn't have a very good singing voice, but that didn't stop him as he loudly sang to the Lord in church.

The last time I saw my dad, he had taken me to the church that our Explorer Post gathered at, as we prepared to leave for our mountain climbing trip to Philmont, New Mexico. When we hugged goodbye, I had no idea that would be the last time I would see him on Earth.

These are just a few random precious memories of many. Dad, thank you for everything. I miss you, and I am looking forward to seeing you again, someday. I love you!!

Richardson Daily News Clippings

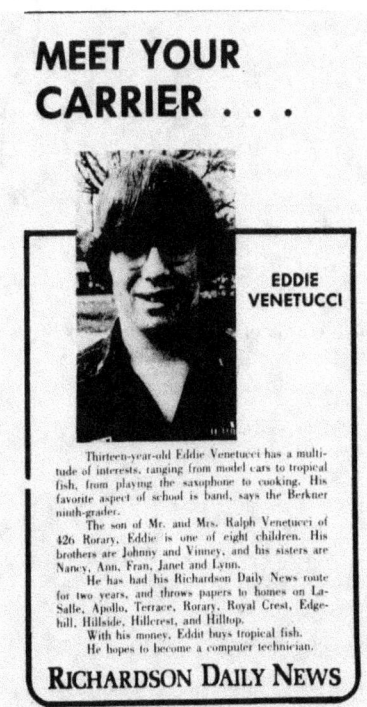

Eddie's carrier article; courtesy Richardson Public Library

Nancy Golden

Eddie is carrier of the month; courtesy Richardson Public Library

Nancy is reading in the lower left photo; courtesy
Richardson Public Library

❧

I was frustrated at how many times we had to move my horse because the land around Richardson was constantly being developed, so I decided to write a Letter to the Editor of the Richardson Daily News, to voice my complaint. While I had a very valid objection, hopefully, I have learned to be a little bit more diplomatic in my later years!

Nancy Golden

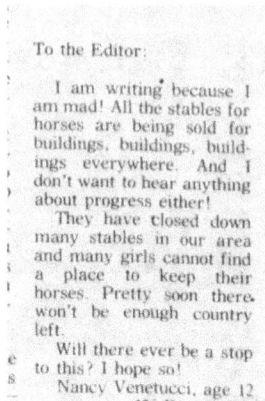

To the Editor:

I am writing because I am mad! All the stables for horses are being sold for buildings, buildings, buildings everywhere. And I don't want to hear anything about progress either!

They have closed down many stables in our area and many girls cannot find a place to keep their horses. Pretty soon there won't be enough country left.

Will there ever be a stop to this? I hope so!

Nancy Venetucci, age 12
426 Rorary Dr.

Nancy's letter to the Richardson Daily News Editor;
courtesy Richardson Public Library

The letter caught their attention, and they responded with a full article! How wonderful it was to be heard!

The Editor's reply; courtesy Richardson Public Library

Eddie and Me: Treasured Memories

Dad, Eddie, and Nancy - Fire truck Christmas; author photo

W hile I miss Eddie a lot, I find much comfort in the memories I have of us growing up together. If you are missing someone you love, I hope you can also find comfort in treasured memories.

Eddie and Nancy visiting Santa; author photo

Growing Up with Eddie

Nancy getting a kiss from Eddie; author photo

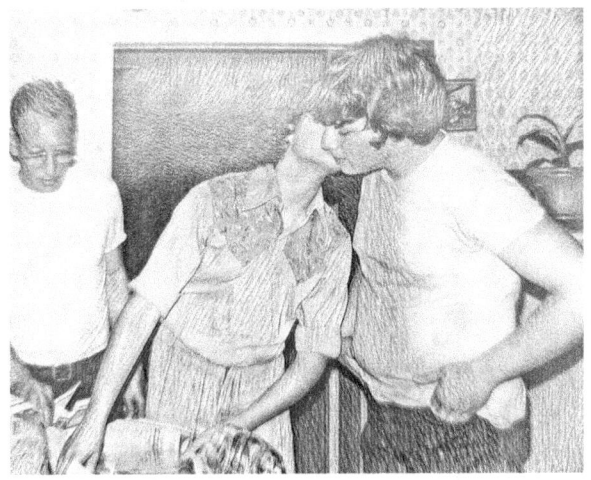

Birthday kiss - Nancy loves her brother; author photo

Nancy with Eddie on his birthday; author photo

Nancy and Eddie; author photo

Growing Up with Eddie

Nancy and Eddie in 2024; author photo

Uncle Eddie holding Nancy's son Joshua; author photo

Nancy Golden

*Eddie, wife Susan, and son Joseph, with Aunt Nancy
holding her niece, baby Jessica; author photo*

*Aunt Nancy, husband Phil, and son Joshua, with nieces
Jessica and Kaylen; author photo*

Eddie's Kids

Eddie, with wife Susan, and their children: Joseph, Jessica, and Kaylen; photo courtesy of Susan Venetucci

Nancy's Kid

Nancy, with husband Phil, and their son Joshua and daughter-in-law Naomi; author photo

Mother-son dance at Joshua's wedding; author photo

Afterword

I intentionally stopped "Growing Up with Eddie" when I did, in early 1978. Our dad died in March of 1978, turning our world upside down and changing our family dynamic forever. Our mom had to deal with grieving her husband, trying to figure out how to pay the bills, and taking care of two teenagers who were hurting and responding in difficult ways. I can't even imagine how hard that must have been for her, and I am very grateful for her strength and love that followed me all of her days, regardless of my sometimes very poor choices.

I wrote this letter to her as an adult, and Eddie's wife, Susan, and my husband Phil both insisted it has a place in this book. I think they are right, because the idyllic childhood we enjoyed was only made possible because of her and my dad.

Afterword

*Mom and Nancy at Los Colinas enjoying an afternoon
together on Mother's Day; author photo*

REFLECTIONS:
SHE NEVER STOPPED LOVING ME

It often astounds me when I think of it. The realization only
hit me fairly recently; such a long time I made her wait for
the appreciation she so deserves. Twenty years to be exact.
Twenty years of unbelievable sacrifice. Of putting others'
needs first, in front of her own. Of giving her time and
energy each and every day, unselfishly. Struggling to give
even more. She is, my mother.

I had always taken Mom for granted. She was always
there for me, so I assumed that was just the way life was. I
had a mother, and it was her job to do all of the things she
did. At least, that's how it seemed to me. Only as I grew
older did that lightning bolt of mature thought strike me:
Mom didn't have to get up early and drive me to soccer
games every Saturday. She didn't have to write to me every

day when I went to Girl Scout camp. Or take me to basketball practice. Or drive ten miles to the stable and ten miles back every day after school, waiting for me while I rode and fed my horse that she and my father had bought for me. And the "didn't have to-s" go on and on. And on.

Mom has given me a beautiful gift made from her love. The gift of a happy, happy childhood. We were a family. I went with mom and dad to my brother's Little League games. My brother sat with my parents at my band concert. Ballet lessons at the rec center. Picnics at the park. Going to the movies to see Robin Hood, even though my leg was in a cast.

One of the most valuable lessons my mother has taught me is, "You can do it." "You can be a good student." "You can be a soccer player." "You can paint your bedroom." "You can do it." And lately, "You can be a writer, Nancy. You can do it." And so I'm doing it. Because I can if I try hard enough. This I learned from my mother.

And then Dad died. What an awful time that was. My big, strong father wasn't there anymore. I missed his bear hugs. I missed his smile and taking his cowboy boots off for him. He had always been there for me. Why did he have to go? I'm only fifteen and all my friends still have their fathers. It wasn't fair. Life wasn't fair. And I'm sorry to say, I wasn't fair. It wasn't the same after Dad died. Wasn't being a teenager tough enough without losing your daddy? Such were my thoughts at the time. Anger built up inside of me, born from a terrible feeling of loss.

Unfortunately, Mom was the closest one to vent my anger on. I was lucky, I chose someone who loved me to hurt with my anger. I talked back to her, didn't listen to her, and finally moved out. But she never stopped loving me. That's why I was lucky. I talked to her occasionally on the phone.

Afterword

She was always concerned about my well-being. I managed to hurt her more with thoughtless arguments, but still, I was lucky. She never stopped loving me. I married without telling her. My older sister finally broke the news to her. The following week, there was a knock on our door. My mother stood there, holding a wedding present. Still, I was lucky. She never stopped loving me.

Time passed, and I finally came to my senses. I could see what I didn't see before. All of the things my mother did for me. A long, emotional talk ended with hugs and tears, and I became a loving daughter again. That was six years ago. We are very close now, and I am very proud to be my mother's daughter. We talk often, just to check up and see how each other is doing. Occasionally, we have lunch together, and I find I can talk to her about my dreams and goals just as I did when I was a child. And she still tells me, "You can do it, Nancy," and I know I can.

I thank God for my mother. I'm really lucky because I know that no matter where I am or what I'm doing, my mother will never stop loving me.

May her memory be a blessing 🩶

Invitation to Faith

Richardson in the '70s was a city of faith where God was still in our schools and our community events, as natural as breathing. When my father died in 1978, we found much comfort in our relationship with the Lord and with the people of faith in our community who reached out to us as we tried to navigate all of the changes. Life can be so hard, and I can't imagine walking through the trials of this world without Jesus.

A family of faith: Mom (Leah), Dad (Ralph), Eddie, and Nancy Venetucci; author photo

Invitation to Faith

Eddie and I were blessed to experience growing up in both Catholic and Protestant traditions in Richardson (along with the Jewish influence of our maternal heritage), and we had many wonderful men and women of God pouring into our young lives. Faith had an important role in our growing up. We were also blessed with parents who had a strong faith in God. Dad would get up early in the morning to pray, and Mom prayed to "The Dear Lord" every night for her children. Although we grew up in a Jewish-Italian household, both of our parents knew Jesus Christ as their Lord and Savior, along with Eddie and me. They are now all together in Heaven, and while I miss them so much, I am looking forward to reuniting with them one day.

In Eddie's last days on Earth, we often talked about how we want everyone to know Jesus as Lord and Savior. We want that blessed assurance for all people! If you don't have a relationship with Jesus, I want to encourage you to seek Him. Jesus loves you beyond measure, and your eternal destiny is at stake. We know we can't go home again on Earth, but we were made to be citizens of Heaven, our real home. Mom, Dad, and Eddie are already in their heavenly residence, and I will join them someday. We want that for you and for everyone!

Your local church stands ready to help you begin that journey. If you need direction on how to begin, you can also email me at nancy@goldencrossranch.com

Acknowledgments

Writing may be a solitary endeavor when putting words to paper, but it happens in community via the inspiration, encouragement, and support of others.

I am so grateful for those who have chosen to partner with me to be a *Light in the Darkness* through my Buy Me a Coffee platform.

My Supporters: Walter, Alison, and Madeleine Brill, Andy Hilger, Donna Hugly, Megan Jackson, Mariia Melnikova, Stephanie Newland, Sharon Pipkins, Ashley Skoczynski, Joseph Venetucci, Vincent Venetucci, Nick and Claire Walker, Bailey Wynne

My Members: Josh and Naomi Golden, Gayle Jones, Mary Oller, Shaun Smith

Their interest and monetary support for Nancy Golden Books enables me to pursue my author career. This book is a direct result of that support.

I also want to thank the members of the Facebook group: Richardson~ Kids of the '70's. Their enthusiasm for this project propelled me forward and broadened its scope. Originally meant just for members of my family, when I asked for help from this group in my research, I quickly realized that *Growing Up with Eddie* had found an audience with them, and the comments they shared of their own memories sparked some of my own. The group Admin, Christy Kelting Radford, was a continual source of encouragement, and the group's excitement for the project spurred me on. Kelly Graf-Perkins, Sandra Hamilton Husmann, and Deborah Nemitz contributed the pictures of swim tags that are found in these pages.

Special thanks also goes to Stacey Davis, Richardson Public Library, Librarian, Local History. I was delighted at her passion for local history and grateful for her cheerful assistance.

Growing up in the '70s in Richardson meant growing up in community, with so many adults at school, church, and in our neighborhoods pouring into the kids around them with their time and care. I would like to mention a few of those folks that I know personally, here: Norman Trout, Melinda Thomas, Debbie Keys, Mary Ann Deans, and Edd Eason. Thank you for caring for us "kids," and making a positive impact on our lives that we carry with us today.

The role of family and friends is vital in all of my writing endeavors, and my husband Phil tops the list. His love and support carries me through when it gets really hard and his wisdom makes each book the best it can be. My sister-in-law Susan has been a source of both encouragement and excitement for this project, spurring me forward to create a legacy we can be proud to share with our kids. I am grateful for my sister-in-law Jane Vaughan; her optimism warms my heart. Joseph Fredrickson's expertise in editing is always a blessing. Daughter-in-love Naomi Golden's cover art captures the spirit of the '70s beautifully, exceeding all of my expectations.

Being an author is hard. Long hours spent writing and researching, with the myriad of tasks that must be accomplished before, during, and after publication. Good friends ease that burden. Many thanks to David and Jan Swann, Scott and Barbara Taylor, Andrea Amosson, and Ross Irvin for always being an encouragement.

Most of all, I am grateful to my Lord and Savior, Jesus Christ, for His loving provision through every season of life.

About the Author

Author Nancy Golden getting ready to work cattle on ranch horse, Barbette; author photo

Nancy Golden wears a lot of different hats—She is a wife and mom, author, engineer, professor, chaplain, horsewoman, and small business owner. She is a follower of Jesus Christ. Nancy is also a member of the National Space Society and the founder of a writing group—the Carrollton League of Writers.

Nancy grew up in Richardson, Texas, and lives nearby in a suburb of Dallas, Texas, with her wonderful husband, Phil Golden, and their lovable standard poodle, Peter. When she isn't working on her next book, she loves to ride bicycles and horses.

Catch up on Nancy's latest fiction writing endeavors and other fun stuff at nancygoldenbooks.com and her Christian nonfiction at nancygoldentakingbackbooks.com

I had a wonderful time writing *Growing Up with Eddie*, and I am very excited to share my stories with you. I hope you enjoy reading my books! If you do, please recommend them to your family and friends.

Being an author is hard work, but it is also a joy. My heart's desire is for the words I write to have a positive impact on my readers and brighten their day–that is my wish for you!

You can email me directly at nancy@goldencrossranch.com with any comments. I would love to hear from you!

One of the best things you can do for any author is leave a review–I hope you'll consider doing so.

www.ingramcontent.com/pod-product-compliance
Lightning Source LLC
Chambersburg PA
CBHW060525150626
46550CB00019B/262